DANCING UNDER
THE MOON

Al Martinez

DANCING UNDER THE MOON

ST. MARTIN'S PRESS
NEW YORK

Design by Glen M. Edelstein

Library of Congress Cataloging-in-Publication Data

Martinez, Al.
Dancing under the moon / Al Martinez.
p.   cm.
"A Thomas Dunne book."
ISBN 0-312-07692-4 :
1. California, Southern—Social life and customs. 2. Los Angeles
Region (Calif.)—Social life and customs. I. Title.
F867.M17 1992   92-4199
973—dc20   CIP

First edition: July 1992
10 9 8 7 6 5 4 3 2 1

Always for Cinelli
Wife, wit, best friend and patient counsellor
and
For my junta of eight, Cindy, Linda, Marty, Lisa,
Russ, Travis, Nicole and Shana
and
For the city room of the *L.A.* by God *Times*
and
(this will do it)
For the *Oakland Tribune,* where they beat the odds

INTRODUCTION

Los Angeles County is a blend of deserts and mountains that embraces nine million people living in eighty-eight cities. Among them are Nobel laureates, porn queens, serial killers, animal activists, priests, billionaires, macrobiotic vegetarians, nymphomaniacs, kazoo salesmen, hug therapists, rap masters, past-life regressionists, and me. I write a column.

I write it for the people who live in L.A. city proper and for those in Beverly Hills, Hollywood, and Malibu. I cover Pasadena and the San Fernando Valley. I drive the winding, high-speed highways of the Santa Monica Mountains and wander through the movie studios of Culver City and Studio City. I dine with famous people at L'Ermitage and put catsup on my eggs with truck drivers at Cafe Mike.

The nature of my columns are sometimes whimsical, sometimes humorous, and sometimes tragic. Occasionally they sing of spiritual redemption, and often they are darkly suicidal. That is because I write about life, death, hope, fear, sex, adventure, happiness, sorrow, frustration, baseball, insanity, and why the Bank of America insists that its women employees wear panties. My wife calls me a drive-by poet.

My job, as defined by my editors, is to put a face on the city. I've been trying to do that, but this is not an easy city to put a face on. Or on which to put a face. On. Unlike New Yorkers, who are all New Yorkers no matter where they live, except possibly for those in Brooklyn or Long Island, we are not all Los Angelenos. It doesn't even sound right.

We identify ourselves by the specific community in which we live. I, for instance, live in Topanga Canyon, not L.A., which is in the mountains between the Pacific Coast and San Fernando Valley. Bob Denver once lived here, and so did Sissy Spacek, Arlo Guthrie, Patti Davis—who used to garden in the nude—Billy Preston, whose dog once tried to chew up my goat, and various other actors, singers, producers, werewolves, writers, and personal-injury lawyers. It is said the Last Living Hippie still wanders the back country of Topanga Canyon, singing, "I shall overcome." He's given up on everyone else.

The best known of our communities is Hollywood. Though part of the city, it is similarly not L.A. It is Hollywood, for better or worse. Hard-drinking W.C. Fields described it best when asked if he ever suffered from delirium tremens. "I don't know," he said. "It's hard to tell where Hollywood ends and the d.t.'s begin."

Hollywood is still that way, though more a metaphor for movies than the actual place where movies are made and stars live. The truly famous now live in Malibu. Prostitutes, punkers and celebrity look-alikes live in Hollywood. Tourists come by the millions to stare at them. Cowboys from Palo Pinto, Texas, and housewives with beehive hairdos from Payette, Idaho. The punkers stare back. Some of them have never seen beehive hairdos before.

L.A. has been described as eighty-eight suburbs in search of a city. True. It is also a microcosm of the world, with all of the world's attendant triumphs and absurdities. We are big, strong, childish, fun, busy, and overbearing. We are not laid-back anymore. We are not mellow.

Our gross product is greater than that of thirteen countries. We are eight hundred square miles larger than Rhode Island and Delaware combined, bound together by five hundred and five miles of freeways on which travel four million cars a year. If we were a state, our population would be the eighth-largest in the nation. One hundred and four languages are spoken in L.A. There is a television station that alternately broadcasts in fourteen languages including Farsi, Tagalog, Samoan, and Rung Hee Rung Zaidi, dude.

You get the idea. Put a face on that, the editors say. Make it part chain saw juggler from Venice Beach, part soap queen from Encino, part low rider from East L.A., part yuppie from Marina del Rey, part billionaire from Bel-Air, part scholar from Westwood, and part superstar from Beverly Hills. OK, they're all here. A little bit of this, a little bit of that.

I call the book *Dancing Under the Moon* because it was the title of a column I liked, contained herein, and because it conjures up what we all are in a sense, dancers under the moon, making our moves and doing our steps with an individualism that makes us perfectly unique in all the world, a little strange but always somehow bearable. So put on your dancing shoes and join me under the moon. It's a great night for a ball.

AL MARTINEZ
Topanga Canyon, California

DANCING UNDER
THE MOON

DANCING UNDER THE MOON

I suspect that thousands of people leave Los Angeles every week to live somewhere else, and on Friday, a day brushed by Santa Anas and laced with falling leaves, one of them was a little girl named Nicole.

Nicole, her father and her mother packed up a yellow Ryder truck and just as the morning was edging toward noon they left for Eureka, where the redwoods reach the sea and the air rings with the clarity of chimes.

They leave our house in the glow and silence of memories.

If you will abide a personal observation for just this once, I'll tell you how it feels to heed the rhythms of life that determine when movement is required; when, quite simply, it is time to go.

Marty and Lisa moved in with us almost three years ago to buy the time required to save money and to solidify their new life together. Into that new life was born Nicole, my granddaughter.

Ours became a house suddenly under siege. I had not even *seen* a diaper or a pacifier or a bassinet for more years than I care to remember, and suddenly I was surrounded by them.

I am, by nature, a tidy and efficient man, easily riled by simple disruptions and driven mad by chaos.

My life, when not occupied with writing, is given over to straightening pictures on the wall, putting magazines in neat piles and picking almost infinitesimal pieces of lint off the carpet.

No one in the whole history of Western civilization has been better at spotting lint.

But babies turn households into shambles and shred with singular determination any inclination toward tidiness.

The presence of Nicole in every room, from toy stoves to small, lacy dresses, could have been the very essence of disruption to a man like me. It wasn't.

There was something special about this girl with the eyes of a pixie and the smile of an autumn morning that almost immediately captured my heart, and as she grew, the attraction increased.

As quick as a hummingbird, as enchanting as a field of wildflowers, Nicole filled the corners of my life with experiences I had not encountered since my own children stopped dragging the cat around by his tail.

Here were my kids all over again in microcosm, learning to walk, learning to talk, reaching toward the upper shelf, trying to sing, demanding the world but settling for a hug.

Nicole is a child of rare sensitivities, as the very young often are, and she defined my moods with a maturity beyond her age. She knew when to laugh with me, when to avoid me and sometimes when to simply touch me.

Moments with her were filled with enchantment.

I saw her one evening on the back deck of our home in the Santa Monica Mountains as she studied the wonder of a starry sky. She looked for a long time and then turned to me and said, "Let's dance under the moon, Grandpa!"

It was a full moon and it lit the night with the kind of secret half-light that illuminates dreams and fairy tales, only half-real and vaguely perceived.

Along with my tidiness goes a reluctance to perform. Dancing under the moon was not high on my list of things to do.

But I was being summoned by a poet who saw magic in the union of movement and moonlight, who sensed the exhilaration of that night and the imagery it evoked.

So we danced under the moon, Nicole and I, me with my clumsy feet and her with her butterfly grace. . . .

Dances end. Moonlight fades. Wind shakes the liquid amber trees bare, and time flickers past like fireflies in the night. Fridays come before we know it.

And on this Friday it was time for them to leave.

I'm terrible at good-byes. My wife is able to articulate all the emotions I am too tongue-tied to express. I stand like a fool in the midst of last moments, hoping the wind that touches their faces will say my love and the sun that shines on their new life will warm their memories.

This is a difficult column for me to write, but write it I must and write it I will because there is universality to the rhythms of life we must all heed, observing rites of passage that clock our rush to darkness.

Our house will be tidy again and the pictures straightened and the magazines piled neatly on the coffee table, but the flow and the magic are gone and that saddens me.

I just don't feel like dancing under the moon anymore.

A DATE WITH SAM THE SYRIAN

Nick Halaby was standing in a cloud of lacquer fumes when I first met him. The fumes were being accidentally blown into the front office of his furniture-restoration shop through an air-conditioning vent that originated in a rear workroom.

I felt like I was breathing through a used paint brush.

"Let's get on with it," he was saying, "because I've got to meet Sammy the Syrian. We're going to Vegas together and Sammy is the kind of guy you don't keep waiting."

"How can you work in this?" I ask, trying not to inhale the lacquered air.

"How can I work in what?" Nick says, lighting a Camel cigarette.

"The fumes."

"They ain't bad," he says, looking up toward the ceiling. "In fact, they might even be good for you."

I am at Nick's place because a friend told me Nick was the best in the business and I have a chair that needs repairing.

When I telephone to ask if he can fix my chair, Nick replies that there isn't anything in wood he can't fix.

"Are you expensive?" I ask.

"I'm nicely priced," he says.

That was good enough to get me to his shop, which is in one of those strip-zoned mini-malls, next to a cleaners that boasts same-day service and a few doors down from Christy's Better Brands for Less.

"You know whose bathroom that was in?" Nick demands when I step in the front door.

He is a wiry little man with the piercing gaze of a chicken hawk and gives the impression that if the question is not answered correctly he will swoop down from the lacquered clouds with talons fully extended.

"Do I know whose bathroom *what* was in?" I ask uneasily.

"That," he says, pointing toward an antique screen leaning against a wall. But, before I can answer, he says, "John Barrymore!"

"Well," I say, and "well, well, well."

Then he utters a sentence so filled with expletives that I cannot even begin to quote it here. If I took out the obscenities only "but" and "if" and maybe "they" would remain.

"I do work for some of the biggest names around," Nick says, gesturing to indicate that they walk into his shop almost every day.

"Marc!" he shouts suddenly toward a back room, "who's the famous broad we do work for? The one who dates Kurt Russell!"

A voice from the back room says, "What broad?"

"The one in Malibu!"

"Goldie Hawn!" a different voice from the back room replies.

"That's the one," Nick says. "What a sweet broad."

Then he mentions Barbra Streisand and Kenny Rogers and someone whose name he cannot remember who used to be president of a steel company, or maybe it was a car company.

"Who the hell knows?" he says, shrugging.

Nick is a second-generation furniture restorer. He learned the business in his father's shop on Brooklyn's Atlantic Avenue and loves the work.

The two voices from the back room belong to Nick's sons, Marc and Jorge, who also do not believe that lacquer fumes

5

are bad for you, although neither of them will go so far as to say they are good for you.

There is a third son, Charles, who is a professor of sociology at the University of Wisconsin and who, Nick confides, thinks daddy "not quite normal."

"He don't understand me," Nick adds somewhat wistfully.

Nick, by the way, is sixty-six but could easily pass for sixty-five. He was born and raised in the Red Hook area of Brooklyn, which, he explains in no uncertain terms, is the toughest place in America.

"I was raised with people like Sammy the Syrian and Jimmy the Arab," Nick says. "I have three sisters, all widowed."

I don't ask how his sisters got widowed because I am not sure I want to know. There are certain questions you don't ask a guy who has friends with names like Sammy the Syrian and Jimmy the Arab.

Nick came to L.A. from Brooklyn thirty years ago, not because of the sunshine and beauty but because one of his widowed sisters bought him a one-way plane ticket out of Red Hook.

"Everyone was looking for me in Brooklyn," Nick says. "I was a gambler. I did horses during the day and floating crap games at night. I was at rock bottom, so she hijacked me."

Nick figures he lost everything he ever earned up through age thirty-five by playing horses and shooting dice. He quit for fifteen years and then went back to it, but quit again. He hasn't gambled for eleven years.

"It's stupid," he says. "I was a sick man."

He is going to Vegas with Sammy the Syrian, Nick explains, only because Sammy is an old friend. He will take in some shows and go to some restaurants, but he will not bet chip one.

As I am preparing to leave, two women come in. Nick turns to talk to them while I inspect an antique desk in a corner of the office.

Nick sees me looking at the desk.

"A piece of garbage," he hollers across the room. "A Mexican imitation!"

"That's the desk you tried to sell me," one of the women says.

Nick nods solemnly, remembering.

"A work of art," he says.

Then he is off to Vegas with Sammy the Syrian.

ALLRED ON A BACK ROAD

This wasn't Gloria Allred's usual posture, sitting quietly in a courtroom off the beaten track, away from the crowds, ignored by the media, listening to herself being berated by another woman attorney more than equal to the task.

The queen of the feminists was accustomed to a different set of circumstances.

One sees her surrounded by television cameras on the steps of City Hall, or in the middle of a press conference outside a Beverly Hills restaurant, lashing the improprieties of a male-dominated society in a moment carefully orchestrated to attract attention.

That's the Allred we know, seizing the day in a flashy red dress, trailed by a media parade she has summoned in the first place, a strident exponent of women's rights, however trivial some of her cases may seem.

Then why does she sit quietly now, demure in a purity-white suit, tight-lipped and nervous as shards of her life are scattered embarrassingly through a Glendale courtroom?

Because this isn't the usual Allred circus, folks. This is quiet personal drama rooted in emotional pain. This is the necessity to clean up when the party's over.

This is the ultimate reduction of a feminist star to very human proportions.

Allred's appearance before Superior Court Judge John Kalin isn't her shiniest moment.

The trial is to determine how the assets of Allred and her ex-husband, Bill, should be divided. That would be unpleasant enough. It is made even more unpleasant by the fact he is in prison for selling bogus aircraft parts to the Air Force through a company he partially owns.

They were divorced shortly after his conviction in 1987, and each is now seeking a share of the other's holdings.

These are messy moments for anyone. The situation requires a cynical assessment of marriage, reduced to components of profit and interest.

The courtroom was almost empty. I sat through a morning of testimony because there seemed poetic justice in the personal travail of a woman who specializes in the travail of others.

Instructed by her attorney not to discuss the case, Allred would only say, "We all have other experiences, and this is one of mine." Her response was muted, her manner reserved.

One couldn't help but feel sympathy.

Allred is wealthy and, God knows, famous, but all that seemed oddly irrelevant in the moment of her despair. I profiled her years ago, when she was still married, and can't help feeling uneasy about the contribution of that profile to her present circumstance.

I characterized Bill Allred as a weak man dominated by a strong woman, and later she joked that the profile caused the divorce. I've never been sure it *was* a joke.

I thought about that as I listened to Bill's attorney rip into Allred last Tuesday.

Arlene Colman-Schwimmer is large, flamboyant and combative, with a reputation as vivid as the floral-print dress she was wearing. She dwarfs Allred both in size and expansive style.

Schwimmer accused Allred of lying to protect her "lily-white reputation in the media" and charged that she badgered her own housekeeper in an effort to keep the woman from testifying.

Allred's attorney, Paul Gutman, dealt with Schwimmer in the way Bill dealt with Allred, quietly and with fatherly patience. By selecting these lawyers, the Allreds almost seemed to have hired each other.

It was a morning without movement until Judge Kalin interrupted the trial to preside over the routine dissolution of another marriage in open court.

Dramas emerge at unexpected moments. While everyone watched, John and Lois Miller were called forward. An almost painfully ordinary couple, they stood awkwardly apart as Kalin asked if divorce was what they wanted.

They said it was, though there was deep sadness to their response. Routine questions followed, and then Kalin said, "That's it. You're dissolved," and in that moment of cold sanction, their life together was swept away like ashes in a gale.

The Millers left the courtroom, and the Allred trial resumed. Gloria watched them leave. I couldn't read her expression, but I wondered if she was thinking about Bill, and I wondered if it was a memory laced with regret.

We are all subject to pain at quiet times. Even a Gloria Allred must answer to the silence.

QUEEN OF THE STREETS

She's a sprightly old lady, barely five feet tall, and probably weighs less than one hundred pounds, but she's found a home on the streets. Neighbors call her the queen.

"I get by OK," she'll tell you, eyes bright, as she dines on coffee and a Mexican sweet roll laid out on the hood of her '67 Pontiac Bonneville.

Inside the car, her mutt, Tweetie, sticks his nose from a window and barks at everything that passes, sometimes turning his eyes upward to yap at the large pepper tree that spreads out above them.

"I go down and buy me a dozen of these sweet rolls once a week for eighty-nine cents," she says, holding one up so I can see the jelly inside.

"I break each roll in half. I have half for breakfast one morning with coffee and half the next morning. That way," she adds wisely, "they last longer."

Her name, she says, is Princess Red Fawn, which is why they call her queen. Her mother was Cherokee, her father Delaware.

For the past three years, due to circumstances she cannot fully understand, she has lived in the old tan Pontiac.

I found her parked under the pepper tree in Canoga Park, the rear seating area of her sedan jammed to the ceiling with boxes and plastic bags.

There are even boxes and bags tied to the exterior of the

car, on top and over the trunk, packed with things, she says, collected over a lifetime.

Princess and Tweetie live in the front seat. She sleeps across the seats and the dog, a brown-and-white collie mutt, either snuggles in beside her or curls up on the passenger-side floor.

"How old are you?" I ask the queen, and she replies quick as a wink, "How old do you think?"

Her face is tanned and wrinkled and her mouth puckers inward to fill the places her teeth once occupied, but even so there is a look of vitality to the old lady.

"Sixty-two?" I ask, giving her room.

"Eighty-four!" she says proudly. "I'll be eighty-four next month." She pauses, thinking. "No, this is, what, August? I'll be eighty-four October third.

"I'm in good health except that both legs went out after that last rain. On a Saturday, was it? I woke up and couldn't walk. But now I'm fine."

She leads the way up the street to show me. Her gait is slow and painful but steady.

"Sometimes I sweep up," she says, gesturing down the sidewalk. "I sweep the whole block."

She owned a used-clothing store once, Princess says, but it was robbed so many times she went broke. She was beaten on the head with a brick in one of the robberies but recovered all right. No one bothers her anymore. She's part of the street now.

"Years ago, I had twenty thousand dollars in the bank and a house in Las Vegas," she says. "I don't know what happened. I woke up one day and it was gone."

She brushes dog air from her black wool sweater. It's a futile gesture. "So here I am."

The queen lives on a six hundred and twenty-three dollar a month Social Security check, most of which she pays to a storage company to keep her furniture.

"You need a thousand dollars now to get into an apartment," she says. "I can't get that kind of money. My husband was killed in the war. I don't know where my son is. He must be in his fifties now."

She chose this street to park because of the shade tree. Also, there are public places nearby where she can wash up and use the toilet.

"I keep myself real clean," Princess says with mixed pride and defiance. She is wearing a spotless red-and-yellow house-dress. "I buy my own soap and take it with me. I wash my dress and then my whole body."

A cop told her recently that she was going to have to move. The queen shrugs.

"I'll just go someplace else. Someplace nice, with a tree."

For lunch lately, Princess has been eating at a nearby church facility.

"The food is real good," she says with enthusiasm. "They put five things on the plate. It's one of those trays with different little compartments. Look at this."

She digs into a Styrofoam ice chest on the hood of her Bonne-ville and pulls out two small cottage cheese containers. One holds a few cold slices of zucchini squash, the other a spoonful of spinach.

"Sometimes," Princess says, "I can't eat it all. So I bring it home."

She puts the food away, thinking. "I have dinner at Biff's. The girls are real nice to me at Biff's."

Only one neighbor bothers her. A woman who runs a nearby shop wants her to move. The others often stop and talk and occasionally give her a dollar or two. Princess uses it to buy food.

"I think it was the shop lady who called the police," she says. "But I don't need trouble. If someone doesn't want me, I'll go. I won't bother anyone."

She hesitates for a moment, nibbling at the Mexican sweet roll. It is on paper towels spread neatly across the car hood.

"I'm no bum," the queen finally says. "I don't like this life, but what am I going to do?"

And, as though by repeating she validates her dignity, adds quietly, "I wash good every night. I'm very clean."

FACES ON THE SCREEN

A friend who lived in Hollywood tried to take his own life about three years ago and failed. That wasn't a big surprise to either of us because he was always lousy at planning things out.

Charlie had taken an excessive number of prescription pills washed down with bourbon and it had made him violently ill. The reason it made him ill, we learned later, was because the pills contained disulfiram.

Disulfiram is a medication used to treat alcoholics. When you take one and then drink booze, you vomit. Ideally, the reaction will cause you to give up alcohol. Either that, or you will spend the rest of your life drinking and vomiting.

Charlie's thinking when he took a handful of the pills was that he would simply float off to eternity and wake up feeling refreshed and burdenless in a place where all is forgiven.

As it was, he ended up in the emergency ward of a county hospital, feeling sick and stupid, surrounded by overworked people who could treat him for his sickness but not his stupidity.

I remembered Charlie yesterday as I watched a student videotape a documentary called "A Journey Back" that dealt with a family's efforts to come to grips with a father's suicide.

The tape was made by one of the man's daughters and won an award given by the Anti-Defamation League of Los Angeles. It said something to me and it ought to say something to you.

Life is short and laughter fleeting.

I don't know why Charlie tried to end it all and, similarly, Louise Gallup never knew specifically why her father, Sam Gallup, shot himself to death.

As Sam's life unfolds in film clips and photographs, we see a boy become a man in easy stages of progression. He earns a medical degree, marries and begins raising a family.

He seems content with his lot, at ease with his surroundings. But is there something in the hesitant smile that suggests life will one day become unbearable?

Is there anguish churning in the soul of the man as he stands by a tent in the rain, looking toward a distant forest? What does the forest hide? What does the smile conceal?

Sam had been an Army medical officer during the wars in Korea and Vietnam. When he returned from Vietnam, he seemed distant and remote.

One son in "A Journey Back" says it was "like someone had poured ice cubes in his heart."

Sam was treated for depression and seemed to be improving. But then one day, a Thursday, he went out into a barn, pointed a gun at his chest and pulled the trigger.

The family was stunned. Why had Sam done that to himself? Why had he done it to them? He had been emerging from the gloom of depression. The ice cubes in his heart were melting.

Then . . . *bam!*

It was only later, Louise Gallup says in her narration, that they discovered why the burden seemed to be lifting from Sam in the days before his suicide.

It was in his journal: "You need to release me. I'll always be a part of you, but I'm getting tired. I feel a strong, silent inner peace I've never felt before. . . ."

Louise says softly, "Dad had already made up his mind."

Charlie was embarrassed about his failed suicide attempt. I'm not sure what embarrassed him most, the attempt or the failure. That's not the kind of question you ask a guy who has just blown a trip to Kingdom Come.

"Boy, was I sick," he said when I visited him in the hospital.

"The pills make you throw up when you drink," I said.

"I know that now," Charlie said. "They ought to sell them

15

as suicide pills. You try it once with those things, you'll never want to try it again."

Charlie was a writer. He reminded me of Oscar Levant, the iconoclastic pianist who spent his life in and out of mental institutions. Charlie even looked a little like Oscar.

Levant, who died in 1972, was funnier than hell and so was Charlie. The night Charlie took those pills, he had me laughing over a short story he was writing about a guy who fell in love with a seal.

"It was those big, liquid eyes," I remember Charlie saying. "But he couldn't take the fish smell and the barking."

Then Charlie sighed and said, "It'll never sell. What you write sells. What I write gets flushed."

I thought about that later and wondered if I had been a reason for Charlie's suicide attempt. By succeeding, had I become the measure of his failure?

Louise Gallup dealt with feelings of guilt by producing a movie that says Sam's death isn't the family's fault. It's a beautiful film, full of love and sadness.

I don't know what happened to Charlie. He left town after the suicide attempt and I haven't heard from him since. I'll miss him. He made me laugh.

RONNIE'S LITTLE SISTER

Two of my friends are psychologists. That's not too unusual, because almost everyone in Southern California is either a psychologist, a psychic, an actor or a hooker. Or, combining them all, a screen writer.

What is unusual, however, is that both of them have expanded their practices out of the hushed environment of their offices into wider arenas of commercial activity. One of them is marketing a stress-relief kit and the other is selling toys.

The one with the stress kit is J (no period) Bartell, a former street kid who discovered along the way that there is more money in fighting stress than in causing it.

His kit consists of a cassette which, through soothing voice and angel music, is supposed to still the mad dog growling around inside you. You roll your head, take deep breaths and concentrate on the center of your body.

That may be a simplification, but simplification is the business I'm in.

If anyone ought to know about stress, it's old No Period J. Now forty-two, he spent his twenties ripping off burglars and dope peddlers, a career that ceased only when a judge gave him the choice of either going to jail or joining the Army.

No Period chose the Air Force, which straightened out his life. There's nothing like military service to kill initiative. Instead of a colorful career as Robin Hood, Jay became a psychologist.

He operates out of his home under a sign that begins, "How To Tell When It's Going To Be A Rotten Day." Two tip-offs: "You call dial-a-prayer and are told to go to hell" and "You call suicide prevention and they put you on hold."

Even psychologists, I suppose, have a sense of humor, however grim it might be.

My other friend is Mike Aharoni, a happy man of thirty-five who used to be my hypnotist.

We met during a period when I was filled with hostility, unlike the gentle, flower-loving pacifist I have become. My family insisted I see someone to calm me down.

First I visited a priest. The session began with an argument over abortion and almost ended in a fistfight. He was Irish, and the Irish are not to be trusted to uplift.

Visits to a psychiatrist resulted in similar disaster. He was a well-scrubbed man who smelled of bath soap and whispered when he spoke. He was either a homosexual or a poet, since those are the only two kinds of grown men known to whisper.

One day he cried. I forget why. But I am not about to pay eighty-five dollars a half-hour to listen to a psychiatrist cry. So long, shrink.

Mike Aharoni was next. I have never met anyone as well-adjusted as Mike. He has a loving wife named Bonnie. He has two loving sons. No doubt there is a loving puppy at home. God has been good to Mike Aharoni.

I went to him because it seemed so, well, *L.A.ish* to have my own hypnotist. He bade me think of blue lakes and green mountains. I demanded to know why.

"To relax you," he explained, smiling. Mike smiles at all times.

"Lakes and mountains don't relax me."

"Then maybe a field of golden daffodils."

"Daffodils don't relax me."

His smile flickered. "Then think of whatever the hell you want to think about," he said. I liked him right away.

His toy store, The Power of Play, is in Sherman Oaks. Two thousand toys, from puppets to chemistry sets, designed to teach as they entertain. A train goes 'round and 'round on

18

tracks along a wall. Mike whistles while he works. Toy Heaven.

"This isn't like stores where kids can't handle the merchandise," he explained. "Here you can touch whatever you want. Go ahead, touch something."

"I don't want to touch anything."

"I'm telling you it's all right," Mike insisted. *"Touch!"*

There seemed a menacing quality to his voice. I have read about decent people who go mad when they turn to selling. I touched a stuffed dinosaur. *Tyrannosaurus rex,* I think it was.

"There," Mike said. "Isn't that better?"

When I was a kid, I played with sticks and boxes, but they too, in their way, were educational. I found a roller skate and built a coaster. I traded the coaster for a football, the football for a wheelless bike, the bike for a BB gun and the BB gun for Ronnie Enos's sister.

Ron's older brother was furious when he heard. He kicked me in the behind, grabbed the BB gun and kept the sister. I learned you can't buy a sister with a BB gun. The lesson has never left me.

On the way home from Mike Aharoni's toy store, I listened to No Period J's stress tape. I rolled my head. I took deep breaths. I tried to concentrate on the center of my body. Then it occurred to me that I didn't know where the center of my body was.

I telephoned J but he wasn't there. So I concentrated instead on a blue mountain lake. An alligator was in the lake. So was Ronnie Enos's brother. I could visualize the alligator moving toward him and suddenly he had the brother in his jaws. I smiled.

There on the shoreline, alone at last, was Sherry Enos. I picked up the BB gun Ronnie's brother had left behind and ran toward her. Now I had it all.

Good-bye stress, hello happiness.

THE BIRD LIVED IN BURBANK

I am sitting there cocking my head and saying, "Hi!" and "How are you?" and "Pretty Katie" just as cute as hell when it suddenly occurs to me, *My God, I'm talking to a bird!*

It is a sobering realization for a man of my attitudes, not dissimilar to the shock a dog must feel when someone turns a hose on him during the act of coupling.

I uncock my head as quickly as social decorum permits, straighten up and get the hell out of there before, awash in sweetness, I plunge into hyperglycemic shock.

Talking to birds is not the kind of thing I do easily. It took me years to get used to talking to babies, and three of them were my own. Only now can I go goo-goo to my son, but he's twenty-seven and not interested.

Being darling to birds, however, is expected of a suburban columnist in an area where men wear red-checkered shorts and women consistently name Phil Donohue Intellectual of the Year.

So, when a publicist called and said there was a nifty story in the Bird Lady of Burbank, I sighed and said all right. I should have been suspicious right away of anyone who said nifty, but the weather's been hot and I haven't been myself.

As it turned out, Lee Whaley is a pleasant lady who really does love birds. I find loving a cockateel a little peculiar, I guess, but then I find owning a goat with a tongue that hangs over the side of her mouth a little peculiar too, and I own one.

The goat's name is Lucy and some years ago a neighborhood dog attacked her, leaving her in the idiot condition previously described. I give her a hug once in a while because the poor, ugly thing cries out for affection, but I'll tell you, man, it's tough loving something with its tongue hanging out.

Lee Whaley has about a hundred birds in her Burbank Pet Center, including the aforementioned Katie, a white cockateel. The prices of the birds range from seven dollars for a lousy finch to sixteen thousand dollars for a hyacinth macaw. Katie is a four thousand dollar bird.

Lee is a middle-aged woman who bubbles with enthusiasm, and it wouldn't have surprised me if at any moment during the interview she broke into song and skipped around the room. I suspect when she was young she was a Mousketeer.

"Birds are in," she said cheerfully, leading me to a back room of the pet store. In the parade with us were Jill Newman, a bird trainer, and the publicist, Nancy Sayles.

"People are changing their life styles and moving into condos," Lee said as we settled. "Birds are perfect for condos. They're pretty, they fly, they talk and they do tricks."

"What tricks?" I asked, remembering a television repairman I knew who taught a canary to change channels on his TV set. The bird and the repairman used to sit and watch "Gilligan's Island" together. It was what they both preferred.

"Watch this," Jill Newman said.

She had Katie wave bye-bye, kiss, spread her wings and show Jill she loved her by tilting her head and covering one eye. I haven't seen anything that cute since Ollie North winked at Sam Donaldson.

"She can poop on command too," Lee added proudly, "and sings 'I wish they all could be California birds.' "

"That's, uh, very nice," I said, wondering vaguely if they were both part of the same act. I didn't ask.

We got into the subject of teaching birds to talk, and Jill said it was pretty much a question of repetition.

"People ask me to teach their birds," she said, "but it isn't worth a hundred dollars to have me come over and say 'hello, hello, hello, hello . . .' "

21

It was then I learned that Nancy Sayles was the voice on a tape that trains birds to talk. She repeats the phrases "sweet dreams" and "night-night" until the bird either speaks or keels over from Press Agent Pathology, which is a disease similar to kidney failure.

Nancy illustrated her bird-talk talent by saying "night-night" a few times, and I couldn't help but think what a perfect job for a publicist, repeating the same phrase until someone, or something, finally listens.

I was taking all this in when Katie suddenly flew over and landed on my foot which, because my legs were crossed, dangled a few inches off the floor.

"She likes you," someone said.

But when I looked at Katie she was glaring up at me with an expression that seemed more murderous than loving. That was when I began talking sweet bird-talk, hoping to prevent any violent behavior on Katie's part.

I do the same thing if I'm in the ghetto and a gang kid begins glaring at me. I rap and break dance until we establish some form of communication and then sneak off when he's busy shucking and jiving.

Ditto Burbank.

After a few bye-byes and nice-birdies I'd had it with Katie and cuteness and wonderful things, so I left. I swear to God, I'll never talk to another bird as long as I live, unless I find one that can sing the Marine Corps Hymn with a drunken lilt. Pooping on command, while admirable, is not essential.

THE COMING OF THE FACILITATOR

In the halcyon days before toxic cheese, tainted watermelons and killer bees, I learned the business of newspaper reporting by covering the Oakland city council. They were a tough, hell-raising bunch who, when they wanted to get to know each other better, usually did so at a downtown saloon called the Hollow Leg.

During the regular council sessions they'd be at each other's throats, but almost invariably they would end up that night at the Leg hugging each other, swearing eternal fidelity and singing "O Mein Papa." That's because a good many of them were, as we used to say, slightly awash in Cutty Sark and water.

They probably drank too much and hollered too much but managed nevertheless to conduct the business of the city with a relatively high degree of efficiency.

Which brings me to Burbank.

The city council there is having a problem because its members, one of them told me, never have an opportunity to get to know each other. So they considered holding a five thousand dollar retreat led by a paid "facilitator," whose job would have been, as I understand it, to facilitate their, well, conversation.

The plan was not dissimilar to Oakland's Hollow Leg Solution, except that now we call it enhancing interpersonal communications, whereas up north they simply called it having a drink. The facilitator was the one who bought the first round.

The Burbank council fussed over whether to hold the retreat, then, at the last moment, voted against it, a flash of wisdom not displayed in West Hollywood, where the council is known for its bitchy infighting. They plunked down four big ones there in order to learn that they ought to get along better.

The legislators in Burbank *do* get along all right, which was what prompted one of them to remark, "If it ain't broke, don't fix it," and led a sucessful effort to defeat plans for the encounter session.

Not everyone was happy by what seemed the cavalier dismissal of modern group therapy. Councilwoman Mary Kelsey said she thought it was a shame and added, "We just never have a chance to sit down and get acquainted."

I asked her why it was necessary to spend five thousand dollars in order to do that. Why, for instance, couldn't they just meet at the Burbank equivalent of the Hollow Leg and raise a little hell? It would not be necessary to get falling-down drunk or even to sing "O Mein Papa," which for reasons that escape me now was the big drinking song in Oakland back then.

They could sip pink ladies and hum madrigals, as long as they had a good time.

Kelsey replied that they were thinking now along those very lines. "We have an all-day session planned October second with the school board to discuss the joint use of facilities," she said.

You get the feeling they might be missing the point in Burbank? A formal session with the school board to discuss the joint use of facilities wasn't exactly what I had in mind.

I'm going to try to explain this in such a way that even a Burbank city council member will understand. In order to get to know each other, it would be best *not* to meet with the school board. You with me so far?

Meet at a nice cocktail lounge in the city and concentrate more on whose turn it is to buy than on the joint use of facilities. The facilities of the joint you're in ought to be enough.

But, Mary Kelsey asked, what about the facilitator? "He is said to be very good at drawing us out in conversation."

I see. Well, Mary, back in the days before group encounters

24

and psychotherapeutic techniques of interpersonal communications, we had something that was probably too simple to be effective in today's rarefied intellectual environment. It was called talking.

Bear in mind, it was an undisciplined and primitive method of getting to know someone. Not until years later did human behavioral facilitators, using advanced audio electronics, evolve the first-approach method of communication that was synthesized down to *Do you come here often?* and *I'm a Virgo, what are you?*

Lacking the wit and refinement of contemporary psychology, we just began babbling away and hoped that the person to whom we babbled would respond in a similar vein.

But how, I hear you ask, do you get started *talk*-ing? Well, a friend of mine who traveled a good deal used to stand up on a bar stool of whatever city he was in and shout, "Anybody here from Oakland?"

He did this in the jungles of New Guinea and, so help me, found a guy who once ran a floating crap game on the east side. They had a great time.

I am not suggesting that Mary Kelsey, a matronly lady in her sixties, crawl up on a bar stool and, waving a tumbler of gin on the rocks, demand to know if there's anybody there from Burbank, but the *idea* is essential to effective interpersonal relations.

In other words, as they used to say around the Hollow Leg, you gotta be loose if you're gonna get juice. I never did know exactly what that meant, but the council members stayed loose, got along fine and probably saved the city five thousand dollars.

WHAT'S SO GREAT ABOUT IT?

I am not one of those who lives on the edge. I do not skydive, scuba dive, wrestle grizzly bears, frequent cowboy bars or reach for anything in my back pocket when a cop is around.

Probably the most courageous thing I have ever done is shout "sex" in a room full of religious fundamentalists, an act which was later ruled unconstitutional by Ronald Reagan's Supreme Court.

I am content for the most part to sit at my little brown word processor and, as a critic once said, fire gob-sized salvos of spit at whatever innocent passersby happen to be in range.

While that may require a certain degree of evil commitment, it does not necessitate risking one's life to satisfy the peculiar tastes of a thrill-seeking audience.

Which brings me to the self-proclaimed World's Greatest Escape Artist.

Steve Baker has lived on the edge for twenty-seven of his forty-seven years.

He has been dropped from airplanes, buried alive, submerged in water, shot from cannons, dangled from tall buildings, set on fire and sealed in steel.

This has cost him a broken neck, dislocated shoulders, fractured ankles, a cracked kneecap and enough pulled muscles, bruises and contusions to satisfy the needs of the most dedicated masochist.

And a fortnight ago, he did it again.

I saw it first on television news. Mr. Escape, which is what Baker calls himself, was about to perform his coffin death trick to publicize a convention of the International Brotherhood of Magicians.

I have known Steve for a long time. He lives with his wife, Julie, in Tarzana, and we meet occasionally to drink beer and to brag, which is the nature of both our businesses. The World's Greatest Escape Artist versus the Bard of Topanga.

The coffin of death trick involves Baker chained in a pine box with forty pounds of explosives atop the box.

At a given signal, a truck races toward the coffin at sixty miles an hour and smashes into it ten seconds later. The explosives go off almost simultaneously.

A split-second before that happens, Steve is supposed to leap chain-free from the destruction, arms outstretched and goatee quivering in conquest and satisfaction.

But that didn't happen this time.

It was only *after* the truck hit the coffin and the explosives went off that Baker came staggering out of the smoke, holding up his blackened hands and then collapsing.

When I saw it, I wasn't sure at first whether he had contrived the near miss as part of the death-defying nature of his act or whether he had actually been injured. Sometimes it's hard to tell.

But later, there was no question that Mr. Escape had come very close, as they say, to buying the farm.

"I was a half-second too late," Baker said from a bed at Sherman Oaks Burn Center, where he lay in pain and frustration. Both hands were bandaged.

"You? *Late?* I find that hard to believe," I said.

"Believe it," Steve said. "When I tried to spring free, I couldn't. Then, whammo."

What happened, he explained, was that the temperature at the site was one hundred and nine degrees. The coffin had sat in the sun for more than two hours.

By the time Steve crawled in, wearing a double fire suit, the coffin interior was boiling. This apparently caused leg cramps and left him springless.

27

"I got out of the chains all right and cleared the coffin before the truck hit," he said. "But my timing was off and the blast caught me. I put my hands up to protect myself and got second- and third-degree burns."

"Maybe it's time," I said, "that you give the whole thing up. You're no spring chicken anymore."

"Quit?" he said, sitting up in surprise. "Are you kidding? This is a boon to my career!"

"But the pain. . ."

"Screw the pain. This was on worldwide television. We're already working on a thirty-minute special about what went wrong. Mr. Escape and the Anatomy of Death, or something like that."

"But you said this was one of the most agonizing injuries you ever received."

"That's what's so great about it. This could be the little push I need."

"Then you intend to go right on being blown up, burned, dropped from airplanes . . ."

"I am not even thinking about quitting. In fact," he leaned close, "I'm working on a new trick that incorporates *everything!*"

"Which means what?"

He smiled. "You'll see."

I don't know what Mr. Esacpe has in mind. I can picture him being encased in concrete that explodes in midair over the Pacific and knocks him unconscious for ten seconds as he hits the water at two hundred and fifteen m.p.h.

Six bones are broken, he is burned bald, his behind is pushed up into his esophagus and both ears are blown off.

He will emerge smiling. That's what's so great about it.

28

SINGIN' THE TACO BELL BLUES

It seemed only yesterday that the Los Angeles school board, in a ceremonial effort to save our children from pimples and rotten teeth, outlawed the sale of junk food in the district's forty-nine high school cafeterias.

Soft drinks were the symbol of evil for the successful good-nutrition campaign, since it is well known that teenagers, when they can't get beer, turn to carbonated colas as their primary source of liquid.

As a result, the board took special delight in singling out Pepsi as the hemlock of the Junk Food Generation and made much of its forced exit from the high school campuses.

Marching songs and folk tunes were heard throughout the San Fernardo Valley as macrobiotic vegetarians and pro-roughage rowdies joined in cheering the school board's decision to toss naughty Mr. Twinkie right out the old cafeteria door and let Mr. Cauliflower come smilin' in.

It was an era equal in emotional impact only to V-J Day and to the come-from-behind World Series victory of the Brooklyn Dodgers over the New York Yankees in 1955.

But, as the song says, that was yesterday, and yesterday's gone.

The board learned two valuable lessons over the period of time junk food was officially *cibus odia* in the school cafeterias of Los Angeles.

Number one, students will not eat where they can't buy

double-dog meat burgers and soft drinks smoking with chemical compounds and, number two, lunchtime concessions that cater to students cannot survive if the students won't eat there.

The cafeterias, as a result, have lost about a million dollars a year in the past two years while places like Taco Bell, In-N-Out Burger, Shakey's and other midday gourmet houses have made a fortune.

Well, boys and girls, it occurred to even the slowest among the school board members that the way to lure kids back into the old cafeteria would be to allow the modified reencroachment of junk food.

Good nutrition flies out the window, you see, when fiscal loss comes truckin' in the door.

So with a minimum of debate, the school board voted Monday to allow carbonated drinks back on the high school campuses, with a finger-shaking admonition, however, that they must be sugar and caffeine free. Whatever other chemicals they might contain are not detrimental, one presumes, to a healthy skin and a plaque-free mouth.

I hung about the Taft High School campus yesterday, near a pizza place called Numero Uno, to determine what the students themselves thought of the reintroduction of Pepsi to the cafeterias.

It took a while to find someone able to communicate in at least simple declarative sentences, but when I did, it was well worth the wait. The student who impressed me most, a boy named Jason, was even able to discuss the subject in abstract terms requiring a less primitive form of verbal imagery, for which I was grateful.

Jason felt that it wasn't fair to deprive a student of his or her basic right to eat whatever he wanted at lunchtime, but when I pointed out that the teenage consumption of Chicken McNuggets was not a guarantee found in the Constitution, he said, well, it ought to be.

We were joined by a girl named Megan with a nice tan and empty blue eyes who said *Jeezwotsthebigdealoverwotweeat?*, which, loosely translated, asks why so much is being made over student comestibles since us-guys are going to eat what we want

30

to eat anyhow. I happen to be fluent in teenage and other obscure dialects of the English language.

Megan was eating what appeared to be a handkerchief smothered with color-boosted catsup at the time, but when I asked her what it was she was unable to say, except that she had purchased it at Numero Uno. Well, it was a tough question.

"Doesn't it bother you," I asked, "to eat something you can't define?"

"I'm doin' OK," she said with a provocative thrust of her hip, a primeval gesture meant to indicate it didn't really matter what she ate as long as her body continued to attract the opposite sex, a theory rooted in the basic concepts that created Southern California.

I for one don't really care what teenagers eat, how they dress or where they buy their Bud Light, and a school district willing to pass out condoms like birthday balloons probably ought not to spend too much time on it either.

The real lesson here for the kids is not, as nutritionists like to say, that we are what we eat but that cash, not cauliflower, makes the world go 'round.

Sooner or later, I'll wager, the school board is going to decide that making money is far more important than keeping students healthy, and the cafeterias are going to start looking like Junk Food Heaven.

No more tuna surprises or mystery meat loafs, folks, but if you can dig color-boosted catsup on a pale tan handkerchief, then, as Megan might say, Wotsthebigdealoverwottlelittlerats-eat?

My thoughts exactly.

A DEATH IN THE FAMILY

You could say of Russ Singleton he was a foolish man who tried to buy friendship with gold bracelets and hard cash and you'd be right. You could also say of him he was a sweet and caring man who gave to others for the simple beauty that giving provided and you would be right in that instance also.

He was, as we all are, a dichotomy of motives and emotions, which would make him by most standards an ordinary man. He was a brick mason who had come by money through no device of wit or talent, but rather through inheritance, a means to prosperity that offers small credit to its beneficiary.

Yet, there was a quality at work in his life that deserves mention here, if for no other reason than the sorrow his death has created on Community Street.

Singleton was thirty-six when he was killed instantly on April 4 in an automobile accident at a nowhere intersection a mile and a half from his home.

He was the only passenger in a car driven by a friend when it collided with another car. Later, healing in a hospital, the friend said: "Russ did everything for everybody. I don't do anything for anybody. Why was he the one to die?"

The comment caught my attention and I found myself exploring not so much the caprice of selective mortality as the feeling that generated the question in the first place.

Who was Russ Singleton and why is he mourned on Community Street?

I found some answers through a man named Bernie Kowalski, who lives across the way from the plain brick-and-stucco house that had been Singleton's home for twenty-five years.

Kowalski had known Russ for all of those years, from the time he was a kid who played on the quiet, tree-shaded lane in an almost rural setting through age thirty-six when he suddenly inherited a lot of money from a father he had not seen since he was two.

It was when the money came, Kowalski feels, that a different kind of Russ Singleton began to emerge.

"He was always a giving person," Kowalski said, "but now he had cash, a fat lump sum and then maybe one hundred thousand dollars a year. He was proud of it and wanted to share it with everyone.

"I told him to get a business manager, to get the money out of his hands, because I knew he'd give it away, and that's exactly what he did.

"Russ would make loans, and when we'd warn him he would never get the money back, he'd smile and say, 'They're my friends,' as if that were the only explanation he ever needed.

"He gave one hundred and twenty-five thousand dollars to a guy named Tom to start a business and, when the business went belly-up in a couple of years, he gave him money to start another business. 'Russ,' I said, 'for God's sake *why?*' You know what his answer was? 'No one works harder than Tom. He just had a little bad luck.' "

Singleton was a bachelor and lived alone, but his house was open to every kid on the block. He even made sure his furniture was strong enough to support them so they could climb on it without hurting themselves.

"Russ loved to give parties," Kowalski said, "both at his house and in restaurants. What was unique about them was they were always *family* parties. He wanted the kids to be there."

Singleton gave more than money, Kowalski remembers. He gave hope to people he hardly knew and, in some cases, free room and board and even an allowance until they got back on their feet.

33

"An example of his giving beyond cash," Kowalski said, "was a gift of expensive golf clubs Russ gave to a boy in the neighborhood. Any guy with money can buy golf clubs and give them away, but Russell went a step further. He *took* the boy to the golf course and taught him how to use the clubs.

"Don't you see? He gave what money can't buy. Time. Himself."

Singleton wasn't pure. He used cocaine up until a year and a half before he died and gave it up only because friends in the neighborhood cared so much about him and gave him no peace until he stopped snorting.

They remember Russ walking in a dream state down Community Street with an old dog named Luke he had saved from the pound and they warned him that if he didn't leave coke alone it would kill him.

Singleton valued his friends and lived for what he could do for them tomorrow, so he stopped snorting, just like that. As it turned out, the number of tomorrows was limited anyhow. All the plans died at that intersection.

A hundred or so friends attended the wake and heard a preacher talk about Singleton as though he were a saint, and then Kowalski spoke.

"The Russell I knew was loud and dopey and crazy and fun," he said. "He was a man who in many ways never grew up, but he possessed a great wisdom.

"He knew that the true gift of life was to give love without expecting anything in return."

I crossed the street and stood in front of Singleton's house. There were yellow seals from the county administrator's office on each door. A wheelbarrow was turned up against a wall. A shovel lay near a hole half-dug.

I stood there for a very long time.

NOTES ON A SLOW DANCER

The impression one gets watching Lynda is that of a sincere, good-natured young woman who is slightly off-balance. The cant is nothing easily discernible as she bustles about the fast-food restaurant where she works, serving and clearing tables, assuring herself with earnest dedication that what she has just done is both correct and complete.

But, still, she seems somehow *different* than the others.

I observed her at the suggestion of customers who said she was special. I witnessed effort not normally found in what Lynda would call "regular people"—those who are not slow learners, who are not developmentally disabled, who are not mentally retarded.

Lynda Marie Rykaczewski is not one of those regular people, and each movement in her life requires a conscious, deliberate decision. Each step is a slow dance, a triumph over the simple routines that others glide over without ever having to consider the music.

By whatever label one applies to her, Lynda has overcome much in her thirty years. The mental handicap is one of them. The murder and suicide of her parents is another, for which she once felt terrible guilt.

It took years for her to overcome the feeling that, were it not for her inadequacies, they might be alive today, but overcome it she did. Life began anew. Her dance under the L.A. moonlight was far from over.

Lynda works at Carl's Jr. in suburban Granada Hills, a fast-food chain that has pioneered in hiring those who are developmentally handicapped. She lives at a nearby state-subsidized home with five other women and their house parents, Edward and Mildred Spence.

The neat stucco house sits at the end of a quiet cul-de-sac and is one of four such places in the San Fernando Valley operated by Kalisuch Homes. They are halfway houses for those unable to meet the demands of independent life, a haven of learning and preparing that simultaneously offers a push and a hug.

There I began to learn about Lynda.

New Jersey-born, she was labeled a slow learner from the beginning. Three brothers and two sisters are normal.

"I just couldn't keep up with the regular kids," Lynda said, sitting on the edge of her bed in a back room of the house. "It was hard, real hard. . . ."

She is a sturdy woman with short dark hair, thick glasses and a smile that flickers like a candle in the wind, caught in a confusion of emotions that sometimes seem to rush her to the brink of tears.

"I found it hard for me to talk like regular people," she said in a voice often so muffled it was difficult to hear. "Words just wouldn't come out like I wanted them to."

But special schools taught her to read and write, and Lynda struggled gamely for her place in an often calloused society until. . . .

The details of that time are blurry. The parents were separated. Lynda remembers her mother showing her papers and documents to give to her aunt "in case something happened."

"In case what happened?" I asked.

"I don't know," Lynda said softly.

The mother had gone to work that morning in a New Jersey department store. Her husband, an alcoholic, tracked her down and, after a furious argument, stabbed her to death in an open parking lot.

The mother's screams were heard by dozens of passersby. No one stopped to help. The case made national headlines,

36

but when the moral clamor had subsided, the fact remained. The mother was dead, the father in prison.

"I felt I was to blame because I could never do my schoolwork, because I ran away sometimes and because I was failing in everything," Lynda said. "I was just too much trouble."

"I hated my father for what he had done. He called me from jail one day and asked me to forgive him but I couldn't. I said, 'I'm sorry, Daddy, I'm hanging up,' and I did. He killed himself a year later."

The children were taken in by an aunt. Lynda was under the care of a psychologist for years before she could overcome the feeling that she was responsible for her parents' deaths.

She tried going out on her own once but failed, then entered an independent living program in Santa Barbara. Four years ago, she came to L.A.

Lynda found work on her own and in June won two gold medals at the Special Olympics, which she donated to a New Jersey high school in her mother's honor.

"I wanted them," she says slowly, "to remember her."

Housemother Mildred Spence believes that soon Lynda will be out on her own, managing her own life, planning her own future.

I asked Lynda what she wanted to do.

"I want my own team in the Special Olympics," she said. "I want to show kids what I know how to do. I want to live a normal life and be a regular person."

Surviving is difficult enough for those with full faculties, for those free of nightmares, for those to whom conquering small details do not constitute a lifetime.

The others take it a day at a time. The music of their lives is tentative but complete. The slow dancers among us teach lessons we ought to learn. They are able, at least, to appreciate the melodies.

IT COULD HAVE BEEN GANGRENE

I awoke one day with the flu.

In a world wracked with pain and disease, that is hardly news, if one is certain beyond reasonable doubt that it is indeed the flu.

But you never know.

My mother used to tell about a friend in Santa Fe who thought she had the flu and it turned out to be gangrene.

"Gangrene has nothing to do with the flu," I would argue, because I was in college at the time and absolutely certain of everything.

"You don't know," she'd say, "you've never even *been* in Santa Fe."

The logic somehow made sense, and I have since accepted that what may appear to be the flu could be gangrene, especially if you're in Santa Fe.

"If you begin to smell like something dead," my mother would say, "you're in trouble."

She had a way with words.

I did not instantly assume I might have gangrene when I began feeling poorly, but since I have inherited some of Mom's tendency toward dire misgivings, I did consider the possibility that it could be something other than the simple flu.

"You smell fine," my wife said. "Lie on the couch and watch cartoons."

"There's nothing on but 'Sesame Street.' "

"Too intellectual, huh?"

"You know how I feel about Big Bird."

"Hang tough. Bugs Bunny is coming up. You like Bugs."

Women don't suffer as much as men. It must have something to do with their ability to bear live young.

When my wife has the flu, she still gets up at five A.M., cleans the kitchen, pays the bills, tends the garden and then goes to work for eight hours.

After work she meets me for cocktails and dinner at Trovare and wonders why the night must end so soon.

I, on the other hand, crawl to my favorite couch and whine because I have to be alone all day.

"Relax," she said, preparing for work on the first day of my illness. "Spend the time resting and cursing Ollie North."

"I'd rather watch Fawn Hall."

"Too bad, poor dear, she's off the air."

As it turned out, no Ollie North either. Reagan's True American Hero was still crouched in the bunker.

So I spent the day pacing and moaning and telephoning my wife so many times her job was in jeopardy. Once in a while, I studied the goldfish.

"You ever notice," I said in one of a dozen calls, "how goldfish will be heading in one direction and then turn abruptly? There's a lesson there for all humanity."

"It's nothing," I could hear her say to her boss. "Just an obscene call."

Click.

Zulema amused me for a while. That is not a Venezuelan hooker, but the hefty middle-aged lady who comes in once a week to clean our house. I enjoy pushing her around.

I may seem egalitarian, but I'm not. I believe God created Americans to Be in Charge of Things, a doctrine which, I might add, enjoys favor in the very highest offices of government.

Zulema doesn't speak English too well, which makes her even easier to boss. It is more difficult to abuse someone who can articulate perfectly their objections to your attitudes and policies.

Sweep the porch. Dust the horse statue. Straighten the doily. Fix my modem. Fight Communism.

She disappeared for an hour, during which the phone rang. It was my wife.

"What've you been doing to Zulema?"

"She's gone," I said. "I think she fled to the Sandinistas."

"She's on the other phone threatening to quit unless I get you out of the house. Be sweet, for God's sake. Or at least be quiet."

"I *am* sweet," I said, watching the goldfish dart abruptly to the left.

Why always to the left?

"She fixed lunch and you wouldn't eat it."

"I hate tuna casserole."

"It wasn't tuna casserole, it was a salmon something. Zulema is a gourmet cook."

"I say it was tuna casserole and I say to hell with it."

Click.

Zulema returned and was able to communicate that I should go to my den and close the door. She did so by the simple expediency of pointing and shaking her fist.

"It's interesting," I said to my wife later that evening, "how primitive peoples are able to communicate their desires."

"What's that smell?" she replied.

I sniffed the air. "I don't smell anything."

"It's kind of a . . . well . . . *rotting* odor."

"What're you saying?"

"That if you're lucky you have gangrene and must be hospitalized, wherein you will be safe from the threat of random violence perpetrated by a wife who *has had it up to here!*"

"The joke's on you," I said. "Gangrene only resembles the flu if you're in Santa Fe."

However, I did decide to spend the rest of my illness in a quiet corner of the house watching the goldfish dart suddenly to the left.

Funny how quickly my smell improved.

LIVING IN AN AGE OF FEAR

I was driving north on the Hollywood Freeway one morning listening to a disc jockey glory in the sound of his own voice when I saw a driver in distress.

That is not a new occurrence on the Hollywood, where motorists are often forced to wait so long for help they must resort to cannibalism in order to survive.

I noticed the vehicle in distress because it was a Lincoln Continental, which is a car generally despised by the hostile poor who use the freeway.

I thought to myself no one is going to help that person because they probably feel he's the rich operator of a sweatshop that exploits and abuses the working class.

Additionally, the Lincoln was on the shoulder closest to the fast lane where there are no emergency telephones, thus increasing the likelihood that its driver might grow old and die before he or she is rescued.

I was in a similar situation once and ended up drinking my own radiator water to stay alive during a summer heat wave.

So I figured what the hell, this might be the time to defy conventional wisdom and assist someone in trouble, even though piety runs contrary to my nature. I took an off-ramp, circled back and parked behind the Lincoln. It had a flat rear tire.

As I approached, I could see that its driver and sole occupant was a skinny, elderly woman with stark terror in her eyes who smoked a cigarette as though it were her last before the guillotine.

She made no effort to lower her window as I stood there with the traffic roaring by. She had no doubt been admonished by her fundamentalist mother many years prior to that moment that strangers were not to be trusted.

As a result, she cringed back from the glass and stared at me in the same manner she might have observed a messenger from hell demanding that she dance naked on the hood.

A lumberjack friend in Eureka used to say that fear tastes like a rusty knife, and I could imagine that the woman in the car was choking on it. I smiled as pleasantly as possible and said through the glass barrier that separated us, "Is there some way I can help you?"

"What do you want?" she said.

"I want to help you," I replied, remaining amiable.

"Why?" she demanded.

"What do you mean *why?*" I said, beginning to feel foolish.

"I don't need help," she insisted. "I'm doing fine."

"I'll change your tire if you'd like," I said, my voice taking on an edge.

I hate changing tires, but no private anguish impedes the charity of a Good Samaritan.

"Don't touch the car!" she said. I couldn't believe the encounter was taking place. I felt like the guy in the cartoon who tried to help an old lady across the street. When she resisted, he beat her up and carried her across.

I stared at the woman for a few moments trying to figure out whether I should argue with her or just say to hell with it and go my angry way. Beating her up, while tempting, was out of the question.

She was trapped in a dread too thick to penetrate, and it was a debilitating condition. Fear clouds the ability to analyze and paralyzes the prey in the path of the predator, instantly decreasing the likelihood of survival in an urban jungle.

The lady in the Lincoln was more to be pitied than despised. The small world she inhabited had become a tomb because the mechanism upon which she relied had ceased to function. There was no adaptability. She was helpless.

"Just sit there," I finally said. "I'll call for help."

I looked back once as I drove away. She was lighting another cigarette and staring at me with the eyes of a gazelle which, for reasons known only to God, had just been spared a lion's killing claws.

I stopped at the first freeway phone and told whoever answered that a woman in a two-toned Lincoln was in dire need of assistance. "Better send a SWAT team," I added. "She may refuse to be taken alive."

As I thought about it, I wondered what could have been going through her head. I don't look like a man inclined to lust or violence. My arms are not longer than my legs and I rarely salivate. My shoes are shined, my trousers pressed and my nose hairs neatly clipped.

"It wasn't *you*," a psychologist friend said. "She was afraid of the unknown, the way children fear the dark. The anxiety was in her own head."

She felt the way we all feel, I guess, when complacency is fractured by the unexpected, leaving us vulnerable to the dangers that swirl like fireflies through the night.

That's why we wire our houses with burglar alarms, why we hire private security forces and why we live behind locked gates.

"I am a party of one," the essayist E.B. White once wrote, "and I live in an age of fear."

The lady in the Lincoln, wrapped in the disquietude of her own making, was a sad footnote to White's truth and a cringing symbol of our own isolation. A party of one, indeed.

RIGHTS OF PASSAGE

High school students in the San Fernando Valley are not known for their willingness to tackle social issues, a condition of lethargy possibly due to the prolonged effect of the sun's rays on their bare heads.

Presidential campaigns hardly interest them at all and the possibility of nuclear war concerns them only to the extent of the damage it might do to either the shopping malls or the paint on their minitrucks.

Then why, you might wonder, do they all seem in such a high state of agitation? Are their earrings too heavy? Are their ghetto blasters broken? Is their pizza too salty? Close, but no cigar. Their proms are in jeopardy.

For those unaware of the Issue of the Decade among the age group that places restraint in the same wretched category as pimples, L.A. school board member Roberta Weintraub has suggested that perhaps one thousand dollars a couple for a senior prom and its attendant "necessities" is a bit too much.

The figure is the result of a study by the district's Senior High Schools Division that found dance tickets alone selling for from seventy dollars to one hundred and ten dollars a couple to cover the cost of a band and a hotel ballroom. Then there are the flowers, pictures, limos, tuxes, dresses, hairdos, manicures, pedicures, parties and trips to places like Palm Springs and Santa Catalina Island.

"It's gotten totally out of hand," Weintraub said the other

day. "The kids are trying to outdo each other. Some are arriving in helicopters. If we were on the beach, they'd be coming in tugboats."

She has asked, therefore, that student committees be established to consider ways of reducing the cost of the Big Senior Night, including alternatives to the off-campus dance.

This has been interpreted by many teenagers as comprising an assault on the very core of their existence. It is especially threatening to those who have spent their entire lives waiting for the bacchanalian delight that has come to symbolize emancipation from the constraints of secondary education.

Some kids will go on to college, of course, but only those who aspire to wealth and power. The others will be truckers and cowboys.

When I telephoned Weintraub to ask if it were true that she is attempting to destroy a tradition as dear to the hearts of high school seniors as Guess jeans and designer condoms, she gasped.

"For God's sake," she said, "don't say *that!* I'm just trying to get some dialogue started, some citywide debate. We could *ban* the prom, but that isn't our purpose. We're looking for alternatives."

Weintraub added that it isn't just the excesses of high school proms that worry her but also a tendency by junior high school students to emulate the worst traits of their elders. She hopes the board will also take a hard look at proms on that level to determine if the empty little dears are similarly engaged in pubescent one-upmanship.

Well, sir.

Not since Coke and Fritos were banned from the campus has anything seemed so threatening to the social well-being of the Valley's high school students. Their telephonic assault on anyone willing to listen makes the Milagro Beanfield War seem mild by comparison. I mean, these kids are serious.

I paid scant attention to the travails of those rising to protest what is already becoming known as the "Prom Bomb" until I too began receiving telephone calls.

One male student named Randy shouted that the school

45

board didn't have any authority . . . I mean *no* authority . . . to deprive them of their right to have fun. He felt it had something to do with guarantees specified under the First Amendment to the Constitution.

I suggested it wasn't his right to assemble that was at issue but the wisdom of pricing school proms out of the reach of all those other kids with similar rights. Randy responded with an epithet that included just about anyone with the temerity to question an activity he felt ought to be removed from the purview of non-participating adults in the first place. Then he hung up.

My high school prom was held in a gymnasium decorated with streamers, but I will not lobby here to limit the crapulence of prom night among those already planning to charter a 747 or to rent the entire island of Maui for their rites of passage. Their parties will end soon enough, as all parties do.

Young people will always test the limits of restraint as, I suppose, young people should. One wonders, however, whatever became of the guiding spirits who are supposed to define those limits, having once tested the borders of good taste themselves?

After learning from the school district survey what the kids are paying for their proms, I think I have an answer. Kids don't pay without parental support and mom and dad aren't limiting anything because it's the parents themselves who, still trapped in a time warp of their own adolescence, are competing at the prom.

And in this area of wretched excess, that may be the saddest knowledge of all.

TWO OLD PALS ON NEWTON STREET

They were riding slowly down Newton Street on a yellow-bright day, two old men on bicycles that seemed almost as ancient as their riders. They moved just fast enough to keep from falling over, and as they pedaled along they chatted amiably, turning automatically down Newton to Lucas and from Lucas over to Macneil, keeping carefully to the side of the road, beneath the shade of the elm and the liquid amber trees.

I was in a hurry that day, charging between offices and deadlines for reasons that now seem obscure and inconsequential. I had come racing down off the eastern end of the Simi Valley Freeway on assignment and was lost in a maze of residential streets when I spotted the old men. They were like living figures from a Norman Rockwell painting, peaceful segments of old memories that touch at the very core of anyone who thinks back to quieter days.

I watched until they turned out of sight, and it wasn't until a week later that I could spare the time to find out who they were, because time races just ahead of me and I'm always trying to keep up.

Their names are Patrick King and Steve Oboski. Patrick is eighty-five and Steve seventy-nine. Both are retired, and both are widowers. They live alone just across Newton Street from each other and have been riding together through the quiet neighborhood every day for fifteen years.

"Sometimes we'll put on coats and ride in the rain," Patrick said, "with the wind blowing." He is a small, fragile man, slightly bent, with white wavy hair.

"The wind doesn't blow as hard as it used to," Steve said, caught for a moment in a memory from his Montana boyhood. "I remember *wind,* let me tell you." He is paunchy and balding and gruffer than Patrick.

They ride an hour or so a day, sometimes in the morning and sometimes, when the heat is too oppressive, in the cool of the early evening. Patrick has a light on his old Huffy bicycle he can turn on if twilight catches them before they reach home. A light and a small American flag. Both men have odometers to measure distance. They've ridden about fifty thousand miles together, talking politics and health. "Discussing our problems," as Patrick puts it, "and yours."

"Sometimes the kids on the block tease us and say why don't you race?" Steve said. "I holler back, 'We are!' "

Patrick added: "Anytime he's out in front of his house when we pass by, an old man we know says *faster, faster!*"

The two old pals laughed.

"They're nice people," Patrick said.

"Very nice," Steve agreed.

Patrick rides a woman's bike because he finds it difficult to put his leg over the crossbar of a man's bicycle. The bike had been gathering dust in a neighbor's backyard when he bought it and fixed it up. Steve rides an old red Schwinn he got at a swap meet. No lightweight ten-speeders here, but ancient pieces of equipment that you have to press back on the pedals to stop. Bikes with balloon tires.

"Steve started riding first," Patrick said.

"I did?" Steve asked, perplexed. "Hell, I can't even remember. I walk into a room, and I forget why I'm there. I'm getting older."

"You've got a long way to go to catch up with me."

Steve shook his head. "I'm trying," he said.

"Well, anyhow, you did start riding first," Patrick insisted mildly.

"That's good enough for me," Steve said.

They ride for health as well as companionship. Patrick to

stay generally fit and Steve to improve the poor circulation in his left leg. "That helps a hell of a lot more than medicine. I don't like medicine. I won't take the damned stuff anymore."

"I'm just grateful that at eighty-five I'm not limping around with a cane," Patrick said. "Steve is really healthier."

"Well, well," Steve said gently, "I'm younger. You're in fine shape. I had that operation just a while ago for . . . for . . ." He paused, trying to remember. "What the hell was it for?"

"I've never known you to be sick."

"Kidney stones!" Steve said triumphantly.

Their goal once was to reach fifty thousand miles on their odometers, Steve, because he sometimes used to ride alone, made it. Patrick is at about forty-five thousand miles. But goals aren't important anymore. Time is catching up with the two old pals on Newton Street. They ride only half as far as they did years ago, maybe seven or eight miles a day instead of the twenty a day they could once count on.

"My only goal now is to live as long as Pat," Steve said.

"One day at a time," Patrick added. "But we'll keep on riding."

"It's like having a tiger by the tail," Steve said. "If you let go, you're done for it."

When I left them, I suddenly realized I was late for an appointment, but it didn't seem to matter as much anymore. Time was a less compelling factor. I kept thinking of those two old pals on Newton Street, pedaling slowly and softly through my memory.

A LIGHT IN THE BARRIO

This is the kind of story we've seen too much of lately: an innocent who gets in the way of raging gang violence and ends up dying in the street.

It happens to men, women and babies, to teenagers and returning veterans, to neighbors and bystanders.

A death in the barrio is hardly a new occurrence.

What distinguishes this one from others isn't only the nature of the victim but the startling heroism of a young woman who put her life on the line to save him.

Where men, out of fear or confusion, refused to risk themselves, she stepped forward, and, so doing, shed light into almost impenetrable darkness.

The dead man's name is Manuel Ortiz. Call the girl Maria.

At twenty-three, Ortiz was one of those guys who shone with a special charm. Not very tall and not good-looking, there was nevertheless a quality about him others found special.

Born in Mexico and educated in East L.A., he seized the American dream as though he owned it. The goal of the dream was to buy his parents a new home outside of the barrio's gang turf, away from the mean streets.

Toward that end, he dropped out of college to take a full-time job and studied at night for a real estate license.

For two years, Ortiz worked long hours and saved money in pursuit of his goal, even delaying marriage to buy his parents their house.

Then two weeks ago, the dream came true. Ortiz announced ecstatically he had bought a place in upscale Whittier. He was going to move in that Sunday to prepare it for permanent occupancy. Sunday never came.

Saturday, July 13.

A party of young people was under way. Manuel's sixteen-year-old brother Jay was at the party. About 11:30 P.M. Manuel came by to pick him up.

Detective Sgt. Michael Lee, of the sheriff's homicide division, reconstructs what happened next:

While dancing, Jay had accidentally bumped into another youth. Angry words were exchanged and a fight started. Jay got out of the building and told his brother what happened.

Manuel counseled him to forget it, they'd go on home. Jay agreed and went back inside to get his jacket. The fight started again. This time Manuel intervened.

He was jumped by about a dozen boys, but managed to break free and run across the street to a taco stand. It proved a false haven.

The group chased him and the beating continued, even more viciously. Manuel was on the ground, unable to defend himself, and though there were people at the taco stand, they sat like spectators at a sporting match and did nothing.

Jay had meanwhile run for help, but it was apparent from the intensity of the beating that it wouldn't arrive soon enough.

Remarkably, a young woman driving by saw what was happening, stopped, screamed for the violence to halt and jumped into the center of the attack. This was Maria.

She tried to pull the beaters off Manuel. When that failed, she threw herself on top of him, absorbing the kicks and punches herself, shielding him from the crazies that surrounded them.

It was an act of heroism made no less heroic by what followed.

The beating stopped, and as two other girls came forward to help Maria pull Manuel to his feet, a killer leaped from the group of attackers and stabbed him eleven times.

Where the beating failed, the knifing succeeded. Manuel

51

Ortiz, in love with life and eager for each day's morning, died ninety minutes later.

Sgt. Lee calls the murder a heartbreaker. "It was a tragedy that never should have happened," he says. "Manuel was an outstanding young man on his way up. We lost a good one."

Five suspects are under investigation. No arrests have been made.

Maria is the pride of the barrio. That isn't her real name, of course. She was a witness to murder. To reveal her name would be to subject her to violent retribution.

Sgt. Lee wants to see her properly credited for the risk she took, and plans to request a special secret citation from the Board of Supervisors. It was an act of courage as real as any that occurs on a battlefield. And make no mistake, this was a battlefield.

If Maria's identity must remain hidden, this at least should be said of her: She heard a cry for help on a night that screamed murder and risked her life to respond.

If there is any hope at all for easing violence in the barrios and ghettos of L.A., it may rest with the women to lead the way.

Let it be said here and now that when it mattered most, a girl known only as Maria was among the leaders.

WHEN THE BOUGH BREAKS

Life, a wise man once said, is a dance on the edge of time.

It ought to be done lightly and with grace, head thrown back, arms outstretched, spinning to a cosmic tempo.

Life is a celebration of self, a solo performance.

I think about this as I wander through a ward of damaged babies in Childrens Hospital of Los Angeles.

They lie in small beds like infants of technology, children of the cybernetics that measure and perpetuate their lives.

Green lines take uneven paths across dark screens above their cribs, red digits flash the numbers of their respiration into a muted half-light.

I see one baby who weighs less than a pound and a half lying motionless in a web of tubes and wires, a human so small he is barely perceivable.

The chance that he will survive is less than thirty percent. The odds aren't good. It hardly ever rains when there's a thirty percent chance.

So welcome to the world of infant junkies.

The babies in this ward are born to the pain of drug withdrawal. They tremble. They vomit. They stiffen. They can't eat. They can't sleep.

They are shaken and twisted by the terrible forces visited upon them in the womb, where their addiction is born before they are.

Cold turkey is hard when it's the first thing you ever do.

This is life, you ask? This is a light-step on the edge of time? Well, yes, it's life, by dry definition . . . but no one's dancing here.

This is a column about drug-addicted mothers who pass their addiction on to the lives they've conceived.

It's about the babies they bear.

You see these women down the streets where crack is dealt. They're wired or sleep walking, selling what they've got for what they can get.

You see them blowing coke in middle-class homes, at parties and sometimes at work.

What you don't see are the babies they bear. They come into the world aching for a fix, in anguish without it.

This is no faint drive, my friend, but a craving that dwarfs the most towering needs.

A doctor tells of addicted monkeys offered the choice of pulling levers for food and water, or for cocaine. They'll go for the coke almost exclusively until they die.

These are human babies we're talking about, not monkeys, and the problem of infant addiction is growing in quantum proportions.

In 1981, there were a little over a hundred drug babies born in L.A. Now there are three thousand a year.

I keep thinking about these babies, the ones who survive at Childrens Hospital by the genius of electronics, and I wonder what survival will mean for them down the long, hard years of their lives.

No one really knows, but a lot of people are concerned. The sins of the mothers are apt to become the burden of society for generations to come.

One drug baby, now twelve, just recently offered a chilling example of the time-bomb effect of infant addiction.

Pushed only slightly he turned on his foster mother and said someday he was going to kill her.

Not much to dance about there.

Victoria Easley got me started on this. She's a reporter for L.A. radio station KFWB who did a series on babies born to drug-addicted mothers.

She called it "When the Bough Breaks."

What intrigued me about it was not the series itself, but the fact that she got involved.

After it was over, she saw at least one need she could fill. She could cuddle the damaged babies.

Victoria formalized a program at Childrens Hospital called the cuddlers program. I heard about it through a colleague.

"This is rare," he said. "How many reporters follow up by becoming a part of their own story?"

Now Victoria and seven other women spend whatever time they can spare holding the babies and talking to them, and hoping by emotional osmosis to provide a will the newborns might not otherwise have.

"We've seen babies with catheters in their hearts improve because they were snuggled," a nurse says. "We don't know why. But we do know that without human contact, babies die."

I walk through the ward of babies. I see the green lifelines and the bright red numbers flicking through the even light.

I smell the hospital smells and hear the hushed footfalls of medical personnel.

These things will stay with me for a long, long time.

Good for Victoria. Good for the women who cuddle babies. And tears for the dances that will never be danced.

"YOU BEEN EATING PEANUTS?"

I took a friend to Kaiser emergency the other night because he had severe and unbearable pains in his lower abdomen. His name is Mark and he's a hypochondriac.

I had already settled in for the night when Mark telephoned for help. He described the pain in throbbing superlatives, which he does quite well, and informed me that, even as we spoke, it was getting worse.

"I'm lying on the floor," he said, with agony creeping into his voice, "writhing."

"Damn," I said, "Dustin Hoffman is on in 'Death of a Salesman.' "

"How ironical," he said. "I'm a salesman too. Do you think that means anything?"

He described the pain again, and I said, "Well, I guess it could be appendicitis."

I was thinking it would be on my conscience forever if I refused him a ride and his appendix burst and he died as I watched "Death of a Salesman." Ironical indeed.

I should have been suspicious, however, when Mark failed to reply to my suggestion that his pain may have been due to a rotting appendix. Normally he would grab at that kind of an opening and run with it like a dog with a bone.

This time, however, only silence.

It wasn't until we pulled into the parking lot of Kaiser that he said, "I'm pretty sure it isn't appendicitis."

He was doubled over clutching his stomach with both arms at the time he said it.

"You're not a doctor," I said. "Let *them* decide."

"I'm not a doctor," he said, "but I do know that my appendix was taken out eight years ago."

"You did it to me again," I said.

He threw back his head and moaned.

Mark checked in at the emergency room desk. I could hear him describing the symptoms of his pain in great detail and so could everyone else in the waiting room.

When he sat down, an elderly lady at the end of our row said to him comfortingly, "It's been going around."

"Not this," Mark said, shaking his head. He repeated the symptoms.

"I had that," a big-bellied man across the room said. "It's diverticulitis, no question. You been eating peanuts?"

"What kind of peanuts?" Mark asked, a worried expression on his face.

"Any kind," the fat man said. "Peanuts get caught in this little outcropping in your gut and then get infected."

A thin, nervous woman who had been listening said, "I've been eating Spanish peanuts."

"That'll do it," the fat man said with authority. "They're the worst."

"I still say it's been going around," the old lady insisted.

"Diverticulitis," the fat man replied indignantly, "does not just go around."

The waiting area was painted pale green, and department store prints hung on the walls. At one end of the room, a television set played a World War II restrospective. A very young Dinah Shore sang, "I'll be around, no matter how you treat me now. . . ."

Hardly anyone was watching the show, however. They were more interested in the medical knowledge being exchanged across coffee tables piled with 1972 copies of architectural magazines and periodicals devoted to air-conditioning repair.

"What do they do for diverticulitis?" Mark wanted to know.

57

The fat man rubbed his chin thoughtfully, the way a doctor might.

"Well," he said, "they give you antibiotics for the infection. You been throwing up, by the way?"

"No," Mark said, then added hopefully, "but I've felt like it."

"Good," the fat man replied. "Probably some diarrhea too."

Mark nodded eagerly.

"That's part of what's going around," the old lady said. "Pain, vomiting and diarrhea. Sometimes there are dizzy spells."

"Maybe you're pregnant," the fat man said. Everyone laughed.

The fat man turned back to Mark.

"If the antibiotics don't take," he said, "they have to go in."

"Surgery?" Mark said. Fear crept into his voice.

The fat man shrugged.

"It's no big deal anymore," he said. "You ever have a gynecomastic tumor?"

Before Mark could answer, a nurse poked her head out from behind a door and called "Robert?" The fat man, whose name must have been Robert, got up and went in.

The old lady instantly said Robert was crazy, Mark didn't have diverticulitis, he only had a bug. But by that time I am certain Mark was convinced he did have diverticulitis and said nothing in response.

An athletic-appearing man who had limped in a moment before said, "Maybe it's colonitis."

That was a whole different kettle of pain, however, and Mark displayed only passing interest. By the time his name was called, he was ready to accept that there was an outcropping on his gut.

He was with the doctor a surprisingly short time and, when he emerged, he glanced at the old lady with admiration.

"What did the doctor say?" I asked.

"He said not to worry, it was going around."

The old lady nodded her head triumphantly. Mark felt better already. I got home just as they were burying Willie Loman.

58

TRUCK STOP BLUES

Every once in a while I weary of the timid collations that characterize L.A.'s pretentious Westside bistros and long for a place that serves chili on its eggs.

I don't want no *foie de veau* and I don't want *ecrevisse de mer*. I wanna dig into a mess o' beans and greasy bacon with coffee strong enough to run an eighteen-wheeler, and then maybe have a chunk of brown banana pie.

For some reason, I can't explain why, I get this urge right in the middle of my aspic salad to say to hell with the bistro and chow down where the truckers eat.

That is not to say they necessarily eat better than everyone else, but there is a kind of reality to a truck stop restaurant one does not feel, say, in L'Ermitage.

You'll find people in Castaic's Cafe Mike, for instance, who don't know a goose liver pâté from peanut butter, but they can kick a loaded semi down the road like a kid pumping a scooter. I like that.

I was raised in a working-class neighborhood where a trucker's status was only slightly lower than a parish priest's. We ate slabs of things in those days, not slices, and poured ketchup on everything from fried chicken to tapioca pudding.

Nothing was left on the plate when we were done eatin' and mama considered it high praise if we gave the bowl a lick when the soup was gone.

I have long since stopped licking soup bowls and I don't pour things from a bottle on delicately sauced *oeufs sur le plat,* but I am not immune to the truck stop blues.

I can hear the air horns blowin' like music down a highway in the night.

I heard 'em for real the other day as Cinelli and I were tooling south on I-5 after a week of visiting family. I was driving her blue Nissan pickup over the Grapevine pretending I was hauling dry bulk out of Delano when she said, "You want to eat at Mike's?"

I couldn't believe I'd heard right. She wasn't raised in a blue-collar neighborhood but in a house with a maid, and would rather dance naked for bikers in hell than pour ketchup on her eggs.

"You were having a nightmare?" I said pleasantly, honking at a guy in a Zacky Farms semi that went rolling by.

"No," she said, "I'm just aware you need your mess o' beans once in a while. Maybe you'd like to stop and get a tattoo first."

What a woman. She knows I like hanging out with truckers and does it for me. Only once have I seen her annoyed in a truck stop. It was at a place near Buttonwillow where a cowboy played "Okie From Muskogee" eight times in a row on the jukebox.

"If he plays that one more time," she said in a voice that could be heard all the way to Tulsa, "I'm going to kick out his lights."

The guy had arms longer than his legs and the look of someone who considered "Okie From Muskogee" a kind of religious anthem, so I led her out before her words reached his brain. Fortunately, that took awhile.

"Did you notice," she said later, "how he growled when he ate?"

Anyway, we ended up at the Cafe Mike, which is just off Castaic's Lake Hughes Road, across from the Country Girl Saloon.

The place has been there for more than twenty years and sees the same truckers all year 'round. Guys like Dixie Doug and the twins, A.J. and Don.

Don, or maybe it's A.J. (they're identical) has a train whistle on his rig and blows it as he drives up. When someone hears the whistle, they put in an order for ham and eggs over medium, because that's all he ever eats.

All you have to do is order the first time you come in, waitress Kristie Gastineau says, and never order again if you want. They'll just keep serving you the same thing forever.

The truckers plunk themselves down at tables or booths and eat with their hats on, the way they do at home, I guess. Then they ask for the ketchup and order food.

I got Mike's Special for the day, two large eggs with chili, beans and tortillas for $5.90. My wife had coffee and spent most of the time watching me eat, the way Kathleen Turner watched Michael Douglas in *War of the Roses*.

Kristie says you've got to have a real good personality to be a waitress in Mike's. She compares it to Mel's Diner in the old television series. "We're family," she says, "and the guys who come in are characters."

They sure are. One of them told a joke about a bullfrog and a duck that still has me laughing.

As we left, my wife said, "Well, did you enjoy your . . . er . . . chow?"

"Sure did, Truck Stop Baby."

"Good," she said. "Now let's kick the rig on home, shall we?"

I got back on to Eye-5 going south, chuckling about the bull-frog and the duck, and imagining I was hauling *veau* on the hoof out of Wyoming.

SOMETHING ABOUT THE MAN . . .

He is sitting in a deli hunched down in a booth under a blue baseball cap that says "Duke" on the front in gold letters. Tufts of white hair stick out from under the cap, making him look a little like a slightly befuddled grandfather in the gently fading moments of his own twilight.

Then suddenly, he begins talking.

Everything changes. The arms move with a speed that makes the air buzz, the eyes glow, the face turns pink and the whole damned restaurant lights up with an energy that crackles around him like the pyrotechnics of a Frankenstein movie.

"I am the last showman," Maurice Duke is saying with a grin that flashes neon. "Everybody knows me! I am an invited guest wherever I go!"

He digs into a plate of prunes, still smiling, still gesturing, still somehow shooting Roman candles over the heads of the breakfast crowd, pinkie rings flashing.

Maurice Duke. He is somewhere between sixty and eighty. Some call him the world's oldest active producer. He has an office at the Burbank Studios and still makes development deals for television.

His career in show biz spans the years from early radio to current film. He has a collection of two hundred hats, plays the harmonica and walks with a cane and a brace because of childhood polio.

"I got polio," he says, anticipating response, "before it was popular."

He doesn't wait for the laugh. He leads it.

"I am the main man," he likes to say. "I am in front."

I heard about the Duke from a press agent named Bob Abrams, who said that among the man's accomplishments were that he taught the waitresses at Nate 'n' Al's to swear and that he produced the worst movie ever made.

Both true. He manages to work an expletive into even the mildest sentence, but it is so a part of the Duke's *persona,* the innate character that drives the man, that the words are drained of their vulgarity.

Because he has been coming to the deli for breakfast every weekday for twenty-five years (surrounded by musicians, agents, network executives, hotel owners and actors), the waitresses began picking up his style of talking and before long were telling the Duke where he could put his scrambled eggs if he didn't like them.

"They love me," he says, waving a lighted cigar around.

They do. There is a fondness for the Duke that is deep and abiding. True, he lends money all over town and always picks up the tab and tips big, but it's more than that.

I suspect it has something to do with the immense amount of energy required to overcome a handicap which, years ago, threatened to prevent him from ever walking again.

The withered legs didn't stop him. A cane and a brace and a specially equipped yellow Barracuda convertible gets him where he wants to go. The energy surging through generates its own will.

"It's the urge to live," Duke says, meaning it. "If you wanna die, go ahead and die! Not me. Not the Duke. I'm still after the young broads!"

About that awful movie. It was called *Bella Lugosi Meets a Brooklyn Gorilla.*

"I made one hundred and three movies, all bad," the Duke says. "But *Bella* was so bad it was camp. It won a plaque in 1958 as the worst movie ever made."

The brain surgeon tries to join us at the booth but Duke waves him off and says, "You'll have to sit with the B-group today." He gestures toward an overflow table.

The surgeon leaves and Duke says: "I loaned him two dollars for a tip once. I told him he could take it off the bill when he did my brain."

Breakfast over, the Duke snaps the leg brace into place and stands. He is just over five feet tall and slightly potbellied.

"The comic Jack E. Leonard introduced me from the stage once," the Duke is saying as he adjusts his suspenders and tucks in his shirt. " 'There's my friend Maurice Duke. He's the only one who walks around with his own erector set.' "

Then he tells about the time, driving back from New York with a friend, where every thousand miles the friend secretly cut a little off the end of the Duke's cane. When he went to use the shortened cane, the Duke says he shouted, "Jesus, I've gotten taller!"

"The thing is," he says, waving to the deli crowd as he takes his leave, "there's nobody left like me, you know what I mean? I am the last of the breed."

I watched him as he struggled toward his yellow convertible, leaning heavily on the cane, dragging the brace, and I thought, *There is something about this man, something special, something beyond the one-liners, beyond the hype, beyond the cigar and the pinkie rings.*

"I've got four development deals going for television now," he says, climbing into the car. "I meet with these baby-executives at the network and they say, 'What's your background?' and I say, 'You first!' "

The Duke laughs loudly, gestures and starts the engine of the Barracuda.

"I'll never be a millionaire," he says, "but I really go, *I wanna live!*"

The convertible peels away from the curb and disappears down the street, and the morning turns quiet again.

I stand there for a very long time. *There is something about that man . . .*

A POPE IN THE NICK OF TIME

With Southern California abounding in ecclesiastical joy, I hesitate to suggest that people who ride bicycles on quiet mountain trails ought to be condemned to hell for eternity, but I'm thinking about it.

It isn't a pleasant concept, I know, and I intended to delay it at least until the Pope left town, but I need the column now, and too much sweetness rots the liver anyhow.

Also, John Paul isn't exactly having a carefree trip when you stop to think about it.

Security is so tight he can't even eat dinner without first having his food tasted by one of the Protestants brought along for that very purpose.

If the Protestant survives after the first few bites, chances are the chow, while not necessarily palatable, is at least safe.

Also, *El Papa* is being bombarded by Jews who want Vatican recognition of Israel, by priests who crave marriage, by feminists who demand new attitudes toward birth control, by Reaganites who want him to condemn the Sandinistas, by dog owners who want him to bless their pit bulls and by nuns who want him to endorse the possibility of a Popess.

Of, if you prefer, a Popette.

Since the visit by His Holiness is not exactly a casual stroll on the beach (he'd have to bless the gangs and the winos to do that), I am going to make a request that while he's in town, he might do me a favor, too.

I was wondering, sir, if you'd mind casting a curse on those who ride mountain bikes in Topanga State Park?

It doesn't have to be a big curse or even a deadly curse, just a little something to remind the damned fools that parks are for quiet walks and not for employing killer bikes to run down middle-aged strollers.

I'm not demanding that they be burned at the stake, just that a match be put to their kazoos.

It's this way, J.P.

Whenever the absurdities of the world begin to assume an importance that outweighs their significance, I meander up a fire trail that takes me to a quiet hilltop in Topanga State Park.

I did so the other day after listening to Gary Hart ask my forgiveness for sleeping with women other than his wife.

I turned the stupid radio off in mid-confession and, later, couldn't even remember the name of the ginger snap he'd spent the night with in the first place.

Was it Fawn Hall?" Tammy Faye Bakker? Jessica Hawn? Corazon Aquino? The entire soprano section of the Mormon Tabernacle Choir?

"It was Donna Rice," my wife said, "although we don't know that they actually, you know, *did* it."

Gary wouldn't say. But since panting and moaning are primary forms of communication for two minds frozen in neutral, I'm sure they at least fogged up the windows a bit.

But then as I thought about it, J.P., I realized that I didn't actually *care* if they slept together, sang together, jogged together or danced naked together on the rooftop.

Having reached that conclusion, I set off for a stroll up the fire trail at the back of my house.

I had not walked a mile when, suddenly, around a corner, came a fat atheist on a trail bike bearing down on me like the devil at a beer bust.

I jumped clear and instantly shouted an obscenity, which is the way my people express their displeasure under pressure.

This so startled the atheist that he went into a spin and ended up, as God would have it, on his fat caboose in a clump of poison oak.

He wasn't hurt a bit, layers of excessive flesh having absorbed the impact of this fall, but I nonetheless inquired as to his health, being a former Catholic with residual inclinations to aid the stupid in distress.

Admittedly, I had mixed feelings when he replied that nothing was broken, but at least I had asked.

Then the jackass began cursing *me* for being in the way of his speeding bicycle and I replied with considerable restraint for a person whose life had been placed in jeopardy that if he kept it up, he would no longer have to mount the bike, it would be protruding from his lower anatomy.

He was bigger than me, as most people are, but I am always armed on the trail with a solid teak walking stick to ward off snakes, coyotes and Lutheran nymphomaniacs, so he simply swore at me again and pedaled on his way.

Since that confrontation, however, I have played bike-dodge with other fools on the fire trails and have learned that what they do is legal.

I complained to the State Park office, but the woman who answered the phone said bikers have a right to be on fire trails, I'd just have to be careful.

When I suggested she was probably less than alert to the danger, she hung up.

I therefore feel, Holy Father, that the only way to deal with the problem is to employ extraordinary means.

I suggest that if you have time between placating Jews, politicians, feminists, priests and nuns, you might give thought to slapping a curse on people who ride bicycles on mountain trails, since most of them are not of the faith anyhow.

If they complain, to hell with them. That would work, too.

BUT THE GOAT LIVED

My wife said to me the other day, "Did you buy the goat grain?"

I said, "What goat grain?"

"I asked you to buy some goat grain."

"I don't remember that," I said.

"You were standing by the refrigerator. It was last Wednesday at exactly 2:30 in the . . ."

"All right, all right. I believe you asked me. But I forgot."

"So now the goats have no grain," she said, "and will no doubt be dead by morning."

I shrugged. "I never did like those damned goats."

We bought them for my son during his 4-H Club phase. Then he discovered women and Budweiser beer. There went the goats.

"That's all right," my wife said, "I'll get the goat grain. You work on your memory."

"There's nothing wrong with my memory."

"Then why," she asked, touching the tip of my nose, "is there a banana on the doorknob?"

Oh, that.

Well, it's just that occasionally I forget little things. The banana on the doorknob was intended to solve the problem. It didn't.

It began when I suffered a leg cramp one day, and someone

said I was potassium-deficient. *Take potassium or you die!* Potassium regulates the heartbeat.

The best natural source for potassium, I was told, is the simple banana. I am a borderline hypochondriac, so I embarked upon a program of eating a simple banana a day for life.

I bought bananas every time I was in a store and placed them in baskets on the dining room table. I bought so many bananas at one place, the owner thought I had figured out a way to snort or inject them.

Every day for about three days I ate a banana. I hate bananas. But I ate them anyhow for their life-sustaining qualities.

Even during the best of times, the length of my determination rarely spans a week. Given a natural aversion to duty, three days was the limit this time. Nature has a way of protecting me from self-imposed obligation. I simply forget what I've promised to do.

The bananas began turning black.

"I won't have rotting bananas in the house," my wife said. "Seaweed was bad enough."

That was last year. A woman we knew was bitten by a rattlesnake and survived without medical treatment. She said she owed it all to seaweed mixed in grapefruit juice.

It was a bad year for rattlesnakes in Topanga, so I decided to try it.

I brought home buckets filled with seaweed and laid the disgusting strands out on the deck to dry. Then I chopped and pounded them into a fine disgusting powder and mixed the powder with grapefruit juice. It made me vomit.

Even blending it with vodka didn't help.

"When life grows too bitter to swallow," my drunken stepfather used to say, "mix it with vodka."

Not this time, Stepdaddy.

"I don't mean to infringe on your health program," my wife suggested, "but if you are going to throw up every time you drink seaweed, it can't be doing you much good."

She was, of course, right. So I began forgetting to drink

my seaweed. It lay in clumps around the house and began to smell.

"One of these days," my wife said as she dumped the last of the miracle snake dust down the garbage disposal, "you are going to poison yourself seeking life eternal."

"The laugh will certainly be on me," I said.

A hypochondriac columnist for the Los Angeles Times OD'd yesterday on powdered seaweed dissolved in vodka. He had been drinking the disgusting mixture in an effort to prevent death from rattlesnake bite. The last laugh was on him. He is survived by his wife and two hundred pounds of algae.

My wife saw the banana venture not as psychological resistance to bananas but rather as yet one more example of my faltering memory.

"You buy all these bananas," she said, "then forget to eat them."

"I forget nothing," I insisted, "and fully intend to eat every banana in the house."

"You won't even eat eggplant because it's too dark. You'll never eat black and rotting bananas."

Maybe not, but I was determined to see the experiment through—regardless of a natural inclination to forget the whole damned thing. A man has his pride.

I bought more bananas, and I tied one to the doorknob.

Its purpose was to remind me, as I left the house each day, to eat my banana.

It didn't work.

My determination vanished like chastity on a water bed, and within two days the banana on the doorknob meant nothing to me.

"I am now," my wife said to me one afternoon, "removing the banana from the doorknob. Any objections?"

I had none.

"By the way," she said, disposing of the banana, "did you remember to get the food for the dogs?"

"Was I supposed to?"

"You wrote it down before you left for work at exactly

70

7:30 A.M. sitting right there at the table. You forgot, didn't you?"

"I should have hung a dog from the doorknob."

"It doesn't matter now," she said. "They'll be dead by morning anyhow."

It's just as well.

THE DEATH OF QUIET PLACES

I used to own a horse named Shorty, which my daughter black-mailed me into buying. Either I got her a horse or she would resist every effort to move from San Francisco to Los Angeles, which she considered the geographic equivalent of hell. She would run away and join a commune that practiced free love or dance nude in a bar frequented by sexual perverts.

Since she was only eleven, it would have been illegal to cast her adrift among the crazies up north, so I bought Shorty, an animal everyone thought was cute. I hate cute.

I was raised in the streets of East Oakland where *horse* was something that junkies injected into their veins. The only pets we kept were dogs and cats. Everything else we ate.

To own a horse was a new experience, and, although Shorty and I were never close, I came to understand how a person might become attached to something without an engine that could be ridden along dirt trails to the quiet places.

Well, I have news. The quiet places are disappearing.

What brought this specifically to my attention was a tele-phone call from a woman in suburban Canyon Country who described herself as a horse-lover. She called Canyon Country *Condo Country* and complained that the land was being bought up by builders who were erecting apartments and condomin-iums where there had once been trees and fields and gentle hillsides.

Almost as bad, these multiple-unit dwellings with names like Live Oak Villa and Wellington Place were attracting occupants with town house mentalities who hated horses and who, as small-minded people will, gloried in circulating petitions that demanded the removal of anything faintly resembling a horse near their stucco enclaves in bourgeois heaven.

The woman who called wasn't just talking about Canyon Country. The same transformations were occurring elsewhere. Freeways, high-speed engines, better housing prices and our almost maniacal desire to *get away* are altering the nature of the landscape north of the San Fernando Valley.

The architects of the new environment are not earthquake and volcano but profit-motivated contractors who measure the human experience in terms of maximum land usage. Without laws, they would build closet-sized condos eighteen stories high in a riverbed that flooded every three years.

I spent time wandering Canyon Country, taking the back roads as well as the main thoroughfares. The woman was right. New structures rise like outposts of a false paradise among ranch houses and old wood frame homes that have been there since the days of the olive orchards.

They stretch from populated districts into the back country and etch jarring symmetrical patterns against the casual beauty of the surrounding mountains. Their pennants flap in a gentle breeze and their fluorescent yellow signs are noisy requiems to the quiet places. *Grand opening! Five percent down! No closing costs!*

A pool here, a spa there.

Well, all right. We all have to live somewhere. I don't blame anyone for ducking the crossfire of urban combat, and God knows you have to go where the price is right. But I keep wondering why the tracts can't fit better into the green country, why greater areas of land aren't preserved for just wandering, and why a horse seems such a threat to the new settlers in an old land that the horses occupied first.

If I can coexist with a horse, you can coexist with a horse. At worst they draw flies, but at best they are evocative of

73

gentler times, those places Glen Campbell used to sing about in the back roads of our minds. Quiet streams and summer memories.

Horse-lovers are militant in the declaration of their rights to own and ride their animals wherever they damned well please. I heard all about their God-given prerogatives and their constitutional guarantees.

But I gained more in two sentences from an old man on a porch swing than from anything contained in the lofty polemics of the horse people.

His small wooden house off Foothill Boulevard resembled a shack from a Norman Rockwell painting. The railed porch tilted on one end, a window was boarded up and the front yard was overgrown. The old man sat perfectly still, observing without apparent interest whatever happened to move across his patch of vision.

I explained who I was and asked his opinion on the encroachment of condominiums in the rural environment surrounding his home. At first he wouldn't even look my way. I rephrased the question. He finally turned toward me but still said nothing. I asked again. Silence.

I was about to give up when he suddenly spoke. His voice was as low as a wind through the trees, a stirring in the mountains, a rustle in the forest.

"It's all gone," he said simply. "Everything's slipping away."

I thought about that all the way back to the office and realized that without saying much, the old buzzard had said it all. The condos are building. The land is changing. The quiet is going.

Everything's slipping away.

WHERE BIG MACS ARE BORN

To the best of my knowledge, the slaughter of a lamb in an agricultural class at Canoga Park High School involved nothing that smacked of pagan ritualism. No students danced around the bleeding carcass, no candles were burned and no prayers offered up to false gods, either secular or celestial.

The process was undertaken as a class project for those interested in animal husbandry as a way, I suppose, of making certain they know where lamb chops come from. They weren't killing Namu the whale, for God's sake, they were butchering a farm animal.

As it turned out, only one student, a young man who wants to be a meat processor, was present at the slaughter, which was conducted in a traditional, if unappetizing, manner. (They conked the lamb on the head first.) A ninth-grade girl who heard about it from a friend extrapolated that into a tale of horror that made the whole thing sound faintly reminiscent of human cannibalism, which, as far as I know, even at its height was never *this* unpopular.

Unfortunately, the story wasn't true. Nevertheless, all those weepy animal-loving people turned out the other day to protest by marching up and down in front of the school. Exactly *what* they were protesting isn't clear; whether it was the fact that the lamb was killed, how it was killed or that a student participated in the killing. There are differing points of view even among those who just love to get out there and march and have a good time on an otherwise wet and dismal day.

I suspect that if the lamb had been drilled by Dirty Harry at the end of a high-speed car chase not a righteous word would have been uttered by those who otherwise fall to their knees in prayer every time a squirrel doesn't make it across Topanga Canyon Boulevard. We tend to dole out our humanity as it fits our causes.

For years I passed a hand-painted sign every day on the way to work that said LOVE ANIMALS, DON'T EAT THEM. The sign, which was finally taken down, was probably put there by a vegetarian stating his point of view, and that's fine with me. I have no objection to anyone living on seaweed salads if the fool finds it palatable.

The rest of us, however, are carnivores, and while we might not eat Old Yeller, we do eat lambs. In order to eat a lamb, you've got to kill a lamb, an inevitability that Canoga Park students are going to have to deal with someday if they intend on being farmers. The only alternative is to eat the lamb alive, a struggle that would probably make vegetarians out of all of us.

A friend of mine, Dale Lowdermilk, puts the whole question of animal rights in proper perspective with his most recent crusade: insect rights.

Lowdermilk is the founder of the National Organization Taunting Safety and Fairness Everywhere (NOT SAFE), a title that he says came to him in a dream four years ago. The idea of NOT SAFE is to lampoon an overreactive society with overkill examples. Hence, insect rights.

"Insects are animals, too," he said to me the other day when I told him about the furor over the lamb. "Just because a snail doesn't scream when stepped on doesn't mean it doesn't feel pain."

Lowdermilk is campaigning for a reduction in the speed limit from fifty-five to fifteen miles an hour as a way of offering bugs a split-second more to get out of the way before they are spattered against an automobile windshield.

While the crusade for insect rights occupies most of his time at the moment, the founder of NOT SAFE is equally sensitive to the rights of larger animals, too. He is demanding, for instance, a fair trial for stray dogs and cats before they are disposed of at the pound. Or better yet, send them as food to starving people throughout the world. Humans, Lowdermilk adds with proper irony, have rights, too. The right to eat is one of them.

A so-called animal activist protesting the slaughter of the lamb at Canoga Park High objected to the students' being exposed to "that kind of violence." Others wailed that it would desensitize the young people to brutality. Since we know now that only *one* student was present, the whole argument could probably be dismissed with impunity.

However, the activists' position does suggest that we protect our young people from the fact that the hamburgers they devour by the millions come in the first place from a dead cow, minus the pickles and onions, of course. Let them grow up believing that there exists somewhere in the farm belt a hamburger *tree* or perhaps a breed of chicken that lays Big Macs like eggs.

On the other hand, maybe it's time for our kids to understand that there are greater truths than those offered during prime-time television, and I recommend that Canoga Park High not only continue its program, but also expand it to embrace yet another fact of violence. Don't simply slaughter the lamb. Kill it in a manner acceptable to the oddly convoluted morality of a double-standard society.

Strap it to a chair in a little room with viewing windows and execute it.

THE MAN WASN'T LAUGHING

An old man walked into a Denny's one Saturday night and could not believe his eyes. Young people were wearing lipstick and eye shadow. Some had spiked and bleached-white hairdos, others had ribbons in hair that was tightened into a dozen different clumps. One wore a dress. And they were all boys.

"What the hell?" the old man said, looking around. "Is there a costume party?"

The waitress shook her head no as she led the old man to a booth.

"Then why are they dressed that way?" he asked.

"I don't know," she said with a bored sigh. "They're just punk rockers. Does it matter why?"

It was the Denny's just off Topanga Canyon Boulevard, two blocks north of Ventura Boulevard. In the morning, it is packed with blue collar workers digging into their ham and eggs and with white collar workers grabbing quick cups of coffee before running with the hours to quitting time.

Even by Denny's standards, it is an unspectacular coffee shop, tucked behind a service station near an on-ramp to the freeway. There is nothing to recommend it as a window on the world of the weird.

Except on Saturday night.

At the height of the weekend, the place turns into a freak show. I don't know why. The people at Denny's don't know why.

It is like cosmic vibrations have drawn the punkers and their camp followers to a middle-American haven where the inhabitants would be shocked the most by young males grinning out from behind slashes of glowing China-red lipstick and thick false eyelashes.

They were inside the place and they were outside the place, clogging the walkway to the front entrance, alternately shrill and hostile, creating an atmosphere that was vaguely unsettling.

I was there for late coffee at the end of one of those kinds of days when nothing comes easy. You struggle for what you get, but what you get is never enough. Nothing sings. Nothing scans. Nothing makes any sense.

All I wanted to do was stare out the window and watch the world go by. Instead I got the freaks.

I've seen punkers before: in their clubs bashing their brains out by hurling themselves at one another in fits of violence they call dancing. Hanging around high school campuses looking for trouble. Strung out and drifting aimlessly, like flotsam on a flood tide going nowhere.

Punkers are part of the contemporary scene in Southern California, the way film celebrities are part of the scene, demanding attention, competing through cosmetics for a place on center stage.

But why Denny's?

The old man, sitting not too far away, asked the question of anyone who would listen, including someone who appeared to be the manager and was busy just trying to get the punkers to sit down and shut up.

All he got in response was what amounted to a variation of the shrug.

Then the old man leaned out into the aisle, turned to look behind him and asked one of the punkers what they were doing there.

The person he asked was one of those whose hair was gathered in clumps all over his head, with a small ribbon tied in a bow to each clump. He sat in a booth with three other punkers and, when the old man questioned him, he just laughed.

It was a pointless kind of laughter, without root and without motivation, and soon he was joined by others at the booth, one of whom shrieked in a range of decibels that hurt the ears.

Their reaction puzzled the old man even more.

"What the hell did I say that was so funny?" he demanded.

The punkers laughed even louder, caught up in their own strange fantasies, removed from reality by the nature of their response, lunatics howling in a grotesque parody of fun.

The old man shook his head and settled back. They were more than generations apart. They were *cultures* apart. They spoke different languages, they observed from different angles, they *perceived* on different levels.

I know that each age has its variation of the punker rebellion. Youth pushes, dares, outrages and challenges through music, dress and point of view.

Change through cultural assault is inherent in the species, an element of the rites of passage that alters the shape and structure of society. The young, like it or not, set the beat and we march to it.

And yet, knowing that, I still find the presence of punkers disquieting. They seem a caricature of change, an extreme to the edge of the abyss where clown-like figures laugh without joy and dance without feeling.

Do they mirror what the world has become? Have we, at last, gone too far?

"This is the strangst thing I've ever seen," the old man said, finishing his sandwich and walking toward the cash register. "I'll be damned if it isn't."

The old man left, and soon the four punkers in the booth left.

And I sat there by the window, staring out into the night. Nothing scanned. Nothing sang. Nothing made any sense.

HELLO, THANK YOU, GOOD-BYE

I have a friend named Travis who is three and a half years old and has begun preschool.

We spent the last weekend of his unencumbered life together and I asked him what he thought of the idea of attending school.

We were walking up a back trail of Topanga State Park with Travis striding along in the lead, as he likes to do.

He shrugged and said nothing at first and, when I asked him again, he laughed and spun around and said, "Hello, thank you, good-bye!"

It's a phrase he uses when he doesn't want to answer, which, I suppose, is better than no comment at all.

Travis is talking a lot these days, and reaching his own conclusions about life in general.

Driving along the other day, I honked and yelled at a man who had pulled his car in front of me.

Travis watched for a moment and said, "He's okay. He didn't mean it."

I stopped honking.

On the weekend, we keep busy. We feed the goats and make spaghetti and read Winnie the Pooh. We also fix things.

Just before we started out on our walk, I was trying to repair a heater fan. Travis watched in silence a while and then said, "It's got a pizza in it."

"I don't think so," I said.

"Yep. Got a pizza in it."

"Everything that doesn't work has a pizza in it," his mother explained. "It's his own idea."

"Well," I said, "maybe it does. I'll have to buy a pizza wrench before I can fix it."

"Yes," Travis said, nodding somberly.

Then he took off across the room, dancing. Amber sunlight splashed through a window. Travis spun across the golden tile like a sun-fired sprite in a dance to youth as old as magic.

Dylan Thomas must have had a scene like that in mind when he wrote about "the wild boys, as innocent as strawberries." A spirit flung free, head back, arms swinging outward, as sweet and natural as a maple leaf in an autumn wind.

"You learn a lot in school," I said to Travis, as we made our way up the trail. The ground was wet after the storm and the air as crisp as chilled champagne.

Travis said nothing, poking instead with a stick at a hole where a spider might live.

"You'll meet lots of kids to play with and make new friends."

"Hello, thank you, good-bye!" Travis said, running on up ahead.

The first day of school is a trying time. We are jerked abruptly from the cozy shelter of home and play and thrust into a strange environment of rigid instructions. The first steps in life are hard indeed.

"What do you want for Christmas?" I asked, to change the subject.

Tendrils of smoke drifted from a nearby fireplace. The smell of burning oak rode down the canyon breezes, evoking memories of other times and other places.

Travis stopped and threw a rock down a hillside. It arced over the green sprouts of new grass pushing up through the rich soil and careened off a wooden fence.

"A fly swatter!" Travis said.

"You want a fly swatter for Christmas?"

"Yes." He says the word crisply.

"Why?"

Travis looked at me. "Swat flies," he said, then went on up the trail.

You don't get a lot of subterfuge from kids. Fly swatters swat flies. Period. Then I remembered. His daddy is death on flies in the house. The son watches. The son copies.

I remember the day my own boy headed off to kindergarten. It was raining that September in San Francisco. He paused at the door, looked back at me and said, "Put my toys away." I said I would. And an infant walked out of my life.

Transitions. Phases.

Travis, when I wasn't looking, had developed a sensitivity I never knew existed. When my wife and I vacationed abroad for three weeks, he felt abandoned. When we saw him, he was silent and distant. It was unlike him.

We talked about it. I told him about vacations and how they only lasted a little while. I told him how much we had missed him. I took him to his favorite place in all the world, Chuck E. Cheese's, a bedlam of electronic kid games.

He loved it all, and before we parted, he said, "No more sad."

He had been hurt by our absence, but now everything was all right.

"Travis," I said, that blustery afternoon on the Topanga trail, "you're growing up. And when you grow up, life changes a little. You do new things. You go to new places. First, you'll find it hard. But then . . . well, you'll like it. I promise."

He stopped suddenly at a point on the trail where the view opens to the ocean. The last of the storm clouds were drifting off like childhood memories. The sky glowed amethyst.

"No more summer," Travis said sadly.

I touched his face.

"Summer will come again," I said. "It always does."

He laughed and ran up the trail and stood on a knoll. That's when I realized, I guess, that Travis, the baby, was gone, and a little boy was standing in his place.

"Hello, thank you, good-bye," he called to the vivid sky.

A wild boy, as innocent as strawberries.

LOVE GRIDS CONNECTED

It was sometime before dawn Sunday when Hoover began barking. It echoed through Topanga Canyon.

I had no idea why he was barking, but I do know that Hoover doesn't bark at just anything.

Old age has taught him that barking reveals his hidden position and therefore makes him vulnerable to attack. Hoover is, above all, a cringing coward.

He crouches behind a bush and only then gives the world hell.

On this particular predawn, however, he wouldn't let up, which led me to believe that he was probably barking at something he felt he could handle. The sudden tinkle of wind chimes, perhaps.

But I couldn't allow the old fool to wake up the whole neighborhood. I got out of bed, grabbed my heavy teak walking stick and headed for the front door in my underwear. I take my walking stick because it is my policy never to face the unknown unarmed.

I opened the door and Hoover bolted instantly for safety in a corner of the living room, which was not a bad idea. Standing at the end of our walkway was a guy in a flowing white robe.

At first I thought it was a spiritual manifestation, but then it also occurred to me that it might be a member of the Ku Klux Klan.

I tried to remember what I had written lately. Had I offended the white folks? Were they paying me a little rectification visit?

If they were out bashing beaners, I was in trouble, so I said, "Hi, I'm Hawaiian, what can I do for you?"

"We're looking for Eagle Rock," the Spirit said. It's up the trail in Topanga State Park. "We think it's a sacred site."

The nuts were harmonic convergents.

I looked down the walkway where the Spirit's followers were waiting.

One or two others were also in white robes but most wore clothing faintly reminiscent of the 1960s, including flowers in their hair.

"You woke me before dawn to ask directions?" I said, shifting my walking stick into an attack position. Even Hoover growled.

"The Galactic Imprint is coming," he said, "and we're lost."

It always happens in Topanga.

Any observance with a hint of mysticism will find the people banging tambourines and dancing naked in the moonlight.

Faith healers, psychics, astrologers, levitating trance channelers, tai chi masters and past life regressionists. We've got 'em all in the canyon.

Sunday was their day. It not only celebrated the harmonic convergence, but also observed the birthday of the Hindu god Krishna and the tenth anniversary of Elvis Presley's death.

No wonder Hoover barked.

I didn't assault the fairy people. Instead I told them where Eagle Rock was and suggested that, if they took the wrong path and fell, they ought to begin humming immediately. They would no doubt float like feathers to the rocks below.

There's something for every decade.

In the sixties, we believed gibberish was a new form of communication. Marshall McLuhan told us that. The oracle of the electronic age.

We read this book then sat around and listened to tapes of squeaks, rattles, honks and the moans of mating whales. A quest for the cool soul of Cosmic Message.

Then Carlos Castaneda came along with *his* book and we were trooping to the desert looking for spiritual meaning in

85

the smoke of peyote. Yaqui sorcerer Don Juan was out there somewhere behind the yucca trees.

Castaneda made a fortune then faded. Yaqui go home.

Now it's Jose Arguelles' book *The Mayan Factor*. New Age visions. Solar resonance. Galactic energy. Planetary alignment. Everybody hum. Everybody boogie. Everybody get down.

Well, all right.

What's the harm? They held hands in Calabasas. They hummed in Topanga.

One man journeyed to the canyon from Santa Monica with two ex-wives and a girlfriend.

"During meditation," he said, "I visualized myself as a love grid connecting with other love grids."

Topanga is probably the only place in L.A. where you can connect love grids and not be arrested. At sunset, they beat drums and banged spoons.

In Thousand Oaks, a hundred faithful *ommmmm*-ed together in a parking lot behind the New Age Center.

"I had my energy balanced," one lady said happily.

Women with dreamy expressions and men with close-set eyes agreed. When it was over, they boarded their saucers and left. I didn't actually *see* that. It came to me in a dream.

Then there's the widow of Sid the Squid.

Her real name is Barbara Fabricant. Sidney, her third husband, was a colorful racetrack tout they called the Squid. When he died a few years ago, they sprinkled shredded racing forms on his grave.

Barbara observed the convergence and the Krishna birthday with a party in her Canoga Park home.

She invited Hindu monks, swamis, astrologers, psychics and the entire Ventura chapter of the Hell's Angels. Only one Hell's Angel showed.

The widow of Sid the Squid was furious.

"Look on the bright side," I said. "You still had the swamis, the monks, the astrologers and the psychics."

"Hell," she said unhappily, "they come by *every* weekend."

Hmmmmmmmmmmmmmmmmm . . .

SUCH GOOD FRIENDS

Shervin Firouzi and David Lowry have the kind of friendship that thrives on simple pleasures. They can enjoy a sunset together in silence, requiring no more than each other's company under a sky washed with pastels.

Or they can just sit and talk about women and life and the kinds of music they once danced to.

Real friendship is that way. It asks little. It gives much.

Forget that the two young men are essentially different.

David, at twenty, is the son of a successful investor and was attending the University of the Pacific up until May last year.

Shervin, twenty-two, an Iranian, came to the United States eleven years ago and was a restaurant worker most of his life, until July, 1986.

David was a goof-off, a punker, a kid in the fast lane. Eleven traffic tickets, five automobile accidents, one car totaled. Three schools kicked him out.

Shervin was hard-working and serious, without a mark on his record.

But they share an adversity that easily transcends whatever they may have once been. Their lives came together miles apart in blinding moments that made them instantly similar.

Both are paralyzed, and both got that way diving into shallow water.

Shervin can move only his head. Without life-support systems, he would die. He can speak, but with difficulty.

David calls himself a "super-quad"—a quadriplegic with some use of his arms. He breathes without artificial support and talks easily.

They met in a convalescent ward at Northridge Hospital Medical Center.

"We clicked instantly," Shervin said.

"This is a friendship that will never end," David said.

There is a special quality to the ties that bind them, a mutuality laced with elements of both strength and dependency.

Like men at war, they gain as much from their fear as from their courage.

I heard of them through David. He called to complain that his friend, a hospitalized quadriplegic, had been denied full-time nursing by Medi-Cal and, as a result, couldn't go home.

His friend turned out to be Shervin Firouzi.

"It's crazy," David said. "He's got to be on a ventilator or he'll die, but they're calling him stable and won't give him a nurse. That doesn't make sense."

Not until he had laid out Shervin's case did David say that he was in a similar, though less severe, situation.

When I heard about the two men, I was as much intrigued by their friendship as I was by their shared physical constraints.

I visited Firouzi first. He sat on a chin-operated wheelchair, a portable respirator affixed to its back. Bright surrealistic oil paintings lined the walls of his hospital room. Firouzi created them with a brush in his teeth. He wants to open his own art gallery someday.

"I'm never going to be a vegetable," he said. "I'm never going to sit around and do nothing."

"He's different," David had said of his friend. "He's gentle, but there's strength there. He's facing things I'm not sure I could."

The strength comes through, both in Firouzi's attitude and in the bold style of his art.

"I've been trying to go home since last February," he said to me. "I have a sister and a mother I can live with. Medi-Cal will furnish the equipment I need, but not a full-time nurse."

He paused, savoring the irony. "They say I'm not at an acute-care level. I'm not sick enough to go home."

To disprove that, Firouzi talks about an incident in July when the portable respirator on his wheelchair failed in the hospital sun room, and the trachea tube in his throat popped out.

"I couldn't breathe, and the person with me didn't know enough about the machine to fix it. He called for help, and a nurse got the respirator going right away and put the trachea back in. If she hadn't been there, I would have died."

A lawyer has filed an appeal with Medi-Cal on Firouzi's behalf. Meanwhile, with David's help, he has turned to the media to tell his story. David's call to the *Times* was toward that end.

I met David next.

After his accident, he was given less than a fifty percent chance to live. Four operations saved him.

"I was obnoxious and undirected before," he said. "The accident woke me up."

David describes Shervin as the big brother he never had. "He's a lot worse off than I am, but he looks out for me.

"When I first got to Northridge, he told me things would be strange but they'd soon get back to normal, more or less. My food tasted weird, for instance, and I kept smelling different smells.

"It was a strange time, but Shervin kept talking to me in that gentle way of his. . . ."

David has been living at home since November. He'll return to school at the end of the month to study finance.

Meanwhile, David champions Shervin's cause even as Shervin acts the part of David's big brother.

They talk every day on the phone and see each other four or five times a week.

"It's not just like a wartime friendship," David said. "It will last." He smiled. "We're too much alike now."

WHEN THE SUN COMES UP

Fear is a compelling emotion. It creeps through a city like fog on a winter morning, paralyzing and infuriating.

It finds enemies where none exist and demands laws that smolder with vengeance.

Fear haunts and permeates. Fear sizzles, burns and implodes. Fear turns us against each other.

Write about being afraid to walk the streets, and the response is instant. Phone messages pile up. Letters clog my mail slot.

An unmarried woman won't date because she's afraid of being murdered.

She has simplified her life into a stark routine that takes her from apartment to work to apartment.

Essential outings are carefully planned for daylight hours. Under no circumstance will she go out after dark.

A man telephones from Fresno and wants to know if it's safe to visit Los Angeles.

Where should he stay to assure safety for his family? Is Disneyland gang-free? Universal City? The beach? *Anywhere?*

Is there, in effect, a manual on urban survival that will enhance his well-being while vacationing in a city once considered so laid back it wouldn't lift its head to watch the world pass?

A letter writer from Hollywood wants more police, a writer from Canoga Park more neighborhood barriers.

Everyone wants a little peace.

I hadn't realized how afraid we were.

What brought all this response was a column I wrote about the tension of night walking and an old lady's fear in her own home.

I wrote about two women murdered in widely separated parts of the county.

I wrote about victims. You, me, our kids, our friends and everyone we know.

The responses ranged from ludicrous to touching, from racist to demanding.

In the case of one of the women murdered, I said she met her death while parked in an area of Wilshire Boulevard known as the Miracle Mile. The irony of death on a Miracle Mile was too disquieting to avoid.

A telephone message was waiting when I arrived at the office that morning. It wasn't the Miracle Mile, said a voice representing the business interests in that section of the city.

Ann Yao met her death *outside* the Miracle Mile. Thank God for that. Too bad about her.

I mentioned that I carried a walking stick when I strolled at night. A male caller said forget the walking stick. He carries a sword.

A housewife from Woodland Hills wants a law passed that would force merchants to hire armed guards to stand in front of their stores like sentinels at Buckingham Palace.

And, of course, the gun nuts responded. *Say the word, by God, and we'll come back with killers strapped to the hoods of our cars!* I'm paraphrasing. But just barely.

The racists had a field day. Blacks were to blame. Mexicans were to blame. Arabs were to blame. Asians were to blame.

Even women were to blame. Didn't they go around damned near *begging* to be raped? You know, like old ladies beg to be murdered and little children beg to be molested?

Can't have people runnin' around begging for pain . . . and humiliation . . . and death.

One racist was blunt. People like me were creating a living hell in L.A. for people like him. Us "Latin invaders" were bringing filth and destruction to the pristine nature of his neighborhood.

91

"Time is running out," he warned. "Do we want another Calcutta?"

Calcutta? Is that near Tijuana?

The most compelling words came from Denise Ritchie, whose nineteen-year-old son Tyge was murdered in front of a Westside deli sixteen months ago.

"Every time I close my eyes I see Ronald Lambakis stabbing my son," she wrote. "I see the blood pour from his neck and I see his face pale and scared and I hear over and over, 'I'm not going to die, am I?' "

Lambakis, a violent drifter, almost plea-bargained his way to a wrist slap. Ritchie fought it. He finally got sixteen years to life.

Since then, she has become an ardent supporter of victims' rights and is working for passage of Proposition 115, the Crime Victims Justice Reform Initiative.

Among other changes in existing laws, the measure would increase the number of crimes subject to the death penalty.

I understand the effort, but that's not going to make us safer.

One hundred and ninety-four people have died in the gas chamber at San Quentin since it opened in 1938, but the murder rate continues to climb with the rising intensity of a scream. Vengeance is a violent, and mostly useless, response to fear.

I have no answers, only questions. I'm hoping for a sunrise somewhere, just like everyone else. Life is getting hard in Calcutta.

THE DAY AFTER

Gordon Dillow was packing it in. Squinting against cigarette smoke and a hangover from the previous night's wake, he hauled stuff off his desk in armloads and put it as carefully as conditions allowed into cardboard boxes.

Once or twice he stopped to study a clipping or a letter. "I don't think I ever answered these," he said, holding up a stack of mail. "I guess now I never will."

Into a box they went, along with pictures, cartoons torn from magazines, a calendar, small gifts from readers and God knows what else. There were two balloons on the wall, one black and one orange, and I wondered if he would take them, too.

For a moment he held up his telephone, considering putting it in a box, and then said, "Naw," and put it down again.

"I feel as though I'm intruding on a family funeral," I said.

Dillow shrugged. He's thirty-eight, tall, Texas-born and looks a little like Ron Howard, the child star turned movie director.

He started in newspapering twelve years ago at something called the Missoula, Montana, *Missoulian*. The *Missoulian?* I thought about making a joke, but I didn't.

You don't make fun the day after a dying.

"We all knew it was going to happen," he said, "but not so suddenly. When I drove to work yesterday and saw all the television trucks parked outside, it flashed into my head, but

I said to myself, 'Please, God, let it be a murder in the city room. . . .' "

We laughed, and then he said, "In a way, I guess it was."

It was Thursday, the last day of the L.A. *Herald-Examiner*. The euphoria that accompanies big events and boozy wakes had vanished from the city room like smoke in the wind.

Robert Danzig's announcement was history, the party was over and it was the day after. Reality was a dull headache and a terrible realization.

The lady was really dead.

Her soul might be rollicking in a whimsical hell for failed newspapers, but sobering incredulity was the spirit she left behind.

There simply was no more *Herald-Examiner*.

I was there on that day after not so much to contribute to the tons of verbiage being written on a newspaper's demise, but to say good-bye to a colleague. I wasn't looking for vast insights. I paint small pictures.

Gordon Dillow wrote a metro column three days a week. He wrote about the city, about his barber in Glendale, about Corky's across the street and sometimes about his wife.

He said I could have Corky's to write about, but he kept his wife and his barber.

"You want this?" he asked, handing me a piece of paper.

It was an announcement of a basketball game between two teams of dwarfs.

"I don't think they'll let me make fun of dwarfs," I said.

Dillow nodded understandingly. "I had a column killed once when I wrote about the *Times*," he said. "I got the paper delivered to the house, but a dog used to urinate on it before I could go out and pick it up.

"I called your circulation department, and you know what the lady said? She said, 'Yeah, that happens a lot.' " He shook his head. "You can't make fun of dwarfs, I can't . . . couldn't . . . make fun of the *Times*."

He paused, thinking. "I guess I'm going to have to get used to the past tense."

I looked out from Dillow's office into the city room as he

94

took phone calls offering sympathy. The cursors of a couple dozen word processors blinked in funereal cadence. The screens were otherwise blank. It was a discomforting sight.

I wondered where the people sat who had brought so much fun and information to L.A. Schwada, Radcliffe, Furillo, Bleiberg, the Krikorians, Fleming, Cusolito, Blake, Sadowski, Durslag, Booe, Koffler, Schwed, Everett.

Where would they go? What would they do?

"You know the most mail I ever got?" Dillow said after his phone conversation had ended. "It was on a column that began, 'I hate France. I really hate France.' It was when they wouldn't let our planes fly over or something.

"The column was reprinted in a French magazine, and I got maybe two hundred letters. One of them said, 'The paper you work for is a towel!' He must have looked the word up in an English dictionary. He meant rag."

Later, we went across the street to Corky's and had a hair of the dog. We didn't do any toasting, but I'll do it now.

Here's to you, Gordie, and to the lady at the party in hell. What a grand and glorious towel she was.

A MEMORY OF DISTANT GUNFIRE

He heard the shots through the blurred perspective of memory, as though they had come from the past and had nothing to do with the present.

They were sharp, popping sounds, and for a moment James Moore sat at the kitchen table, staring and trying to figure out if they were real.

It was late afternoon, and a pale sunlight washed the room with faint shadows. Food cooked on the stove of the tidy West Compton home. Traffic hummed on nearby Redondo Beach Boulevard.

The time required for Moore to separate reality from memory was the blink of an eye, but it seemed forever. When the separation occurred, it was a thunderclap.

Moore bolted out the back door, down the stairs and toward the fence, his brain reprocessing the echo of three gunshots, gauging their direction, placing his young son in the vicinity, screaming *not again!*

When he reached the fence he shouted, "Gregory!" and almost instantaneously saw his son and two companions on the ground . . . then rising and running toward him, unhurt.

Another drive-by shooting, his brain said.

Moore closed his eyes. It was then, he says, that it all came rushing back . . .

Three years ago, he and his wife, Ceola, were at the same kitchen table, having a last cup of coffee. It was 4 A.M. A night of family card playing had ended. The children were in bed.

"We were just sitting here talking," Moore said. "All of a sudden, bam, bam! I turned to her and said, 'Ceola, you hear that?' "

Moore's wife of twenty years didn't answer. One of the two bullets fired at random toward their corner house had pierced her skull. She was brain dead by the time she slumped forward. She stopped breathing several hours later.

A drive-by shooting with no specific victim in mind, a bullet fired toward a light in a window, had claimed the wife Moore loved beyond measure.

"I was just getting over it," he said the other day as we sat at the same kitchen table, "when the other shooting happened."

He is a fifty-year-old black man who could pass for forty. For the last twenty years he has worked as a lab technician at the B.F. Goodrich Chemical Co. Ceola had been a nursery school teacher and an active church member.

"All the emotions I felt when she was killed came back to me," Moore said. "I felt grief and fear and anger. Now I'm just plain angry. This is no kind of life! What the hell is going on?"

It was the same question I asked as I drove through his neighborhood of neat homes and mowed lawns, of trimmed hedges and fresh paint.

Pride had gone into this neighborhood. Care had gone into it. A young man worked on his car. Children played under shade trees. Neighbors stopped to talk to each other. Stanford Street deserved better than gunfire.

"What kind of existence is it sitting here every day waiting for something to happen?" Moore said, nervously lighting a cigarette. "Everybody is sick of it. It's getting like the Wild West.

"The kids are scared to death and beginning to carry guns for defense. But one thing leads to another. Where does defense end and offense begin? I wake up every night, listening. . . ."

Three of Moore's children were living at home when his wife

was killed. Dennis, twenty-two, has since moved away. Gregory, nineteen, and Rhonda, fourteen, are still there.

Five gang members were arrested after the shooting two weeks ago. No one has ever been arrested in Ceola's murder.

To the best of Moore's knowledge, the shooting that took her life was the first in the neighborhood, but since then there have been at least three others, one of which wounded a young boy.

Gang graffiti proliferates on the edges of Stanford Street. Drug dealers clog Visalia Avenue.

"I've gone down there and watched them deal," Moore said. "They're blond and blue-eyed people, obviously not from around here. I'd take down license numbers and be more a vigilante, but suppose they track me down and go after my kids?"

Moore is trying to unite the neighborhood to somehow solve the problem. He's asking for more random patrols by sheriff's deputies, but he's not sure they're that interested in helping.

"The night my wife was killed," he said, "I heard one of the detectives say, 'Just another shitty day in the ghetto.' Does that sound like they care?"

James Moore won't run. The house he has lived in for ten years is the house his wife chose, and her memory is still bright. But the question he asks is the question we all ought to ponder.

Will it ever be safe again?

BARNUM, BAIL AND SHOW BIZ

Trust me when I tell you that Giuseppe Mariano Roselli, ex-pugilist and self-proclaimed bail bondsman to the stars, is about to become more popular than linguine and clams.

You will see him one of these days on the Johnny Carson show, his diamond-and-gold boxing-glove necklace gleaming in the stage lights, and you will hear him on the Michael Jackson show, telling about the time he dressed in drag to nail a guy who owned him money.

You know him as Joey Barnum, a lightweight contender in the 1940s who, after his retirement, came back to beat the fighter he was managing.

A television series based on Joey is in the works, and a book is in its final stages. The kid from Chicago's Little Sicily is gonna be a star.

I learned this first-hand from Joey himself, and from his partner, Joe Seide, ex-client, ex-con and ex-press agent. I had seen Joey's picture in the paper with Milton Berle at a restaurant opening and wanted to know more about him.

We met in his office across the street from the courthouse in El Monte. Joey is resplendent in tailor-made clothes, eight hundred dollar snakeskin boots and a thirty-five hundred dollar Rolex watch.

He looks at the world through rose-tinted glasses and, because his designer shirt is open halfway to his stomach, the boxing glove necklace gleams like a logo of his life.

If everything goes right, the TV series will be like the old "Barney Miller" show, but centered on the bail bond business, which Joey has been involved in for twenty-seven years.

Mickey Cohen's bail bondsman taught Joey the business in which he now prevails. His license plate used to say EX PUG. Now it says MR BAIL.

Joey is no shrinking violet.

An entire wall of his office is filled with pictures of himself with celebrities you'll probably never meet, even if they were still alive.

Marilyn Monroe, for instance, was a good friend, William Devane is a fan and Joey dines occasionally with Jackie Stallone at Matteo's.

In fact, her son Sly phoned when I was in the office, but Joey was in no hurry to answer. By the time he did, Stallone had hung up.

Joey doubled for John Garfield in the movie *Body and Soul,* and a television film, "The Killer Instinct," was based on the kid's life.

He got to know people in show biz through his peripheral involvement, and later as he "serviced" them. Big Names have called upon Joey to bail them out of the slammer.

One of those Big Names got in trouble once by failing to pay a loan shark. Three "collectors" came to call. Joey, who is as hard and lean as he was forty years ago, stepped between the Big Name and the collectors. They recognized him and backed off. The man must have finally paid because he's still alive.

"Joey's a real colorful character," Joe Seide says, shaking his head. Seide did eighteen months in federal prison for income tax evasion. A big man, he dominates the conversation.

"The business," Joey manages to say, "is not all dark. One time. . . ."

"Oh, yeah," Seide says, anticipating the story. "A client stiffs Joey and. . . ."

"Wait," Joey says in a commanding voice. "I'll tell."

It's a terrific story. Joey dressed up in women's clothing to catch a guy who had jumped bail. A tipster said the guy had a gun, so going in drag was a way for Joey to disguise himself.

"I find him at a bar," Joey says, "and sidle up to him. I must look pretty good, because he buys me a drink. I spill the drink on his lap, and when he's bending over to wipe it up, I hit him with a left hook and a right cross and he goes down like a tree.

"The bartender stares and says, 'Man, can that broad hit!' "

Joey's got a lot of stories, some of which will never be told in explicit detail in what is known as a Family Newspaper: like the nut who was cursing the pay phone outside Joey's office for stealing his quarter.

Joey was watching and dialed the number of the pay phone. When the nut answered, Joey cursed him back in his own terms, and the guy was so startled he took off like the devil himself was in pursuit.

Barnum's office glows with memorabilia of his boxing career, from an oil painting to an old poster. He had a clock that rang a boxing bell every thirty minutes, and tells about the punchy ex-fighter who dropped by, heard the bell, slumped back in a chair and asked for water.

"What worried me," Joey says, "is that the guy was so punchy he could hardly talk, but I understood him."

Joe Seide laughs like crazy and says, "What a colorful guy."

Mr. Bail, about to become famous, smiles.

A SOFT RAIN FALLING

A soft rain was falling the day the Old Lady died. It misted the windshields of the cars on Wilshire and dampened the walkways used by those who had come to say good-bye. Reporters and photographers were still there when I arrived because this was an event of significance in Los Angeles, the death of a queen called the Ambassador Hotel, a part of our past that danced all night.

I had not intended to witness its final closing because the affair promised to be exactly what it was, a story on every front page, a segment on every television news show, a report on every radio station. It seemed to me everyone would have had enough of the Ambassador by the time I got around to saying anything.

There was another reason to avoid the whole thing. You can talk all you want about who occupied the celebrity suites and who played the Cocoanut Grove, but the image of the Ambassador that haunts the memory is that of Bobby Kennedy lying on the kitchen floor, staring brain-dead at the ceiling.

I recall with terrible clarity the night he died. I sat alone in a darkened room of my home in the Berkeley hills watching the televised news reports, seeing the same scenes over and over again, thinking that this couldn't be happening to us, all this horror, and watching it finally without sound, as the murder played in pantomime until dawn.

This was on my mind Tuesday when the Ambassador

checked out its last guest, shut down its gift shop and began carting away the accouterments of commerce. But then I heard someone in the city room refer to the hotel as "the Old Lady," and the phrase evoked a different kind of imagery, the one I was talking about earlier, when the Lady was young and wore rhinestones.

It couldn't hurt to stop by. I was on my way to Beaufait Avenue in the San Fernando Valley to look at the homes that had been destroyed in last December's brush fires because the idea of caprice, of random selection, has always fascinated me. What spared one home and burned the other? Why hadn't it rained sooner? By whose hand are we nudged along the road to Armageddon?

The Ambassador isn't exactly on the route to Beaufait, but I'd compromise. A quick look at the grand dame in her dated finery (one imagines sequins and flowing gowns) and then off to areas of more compelling attention, the firebombed homes that lay like skeletons in the rain along the charred northern rim of the Valley.

I had only been in the hotel a little while when I met A. Lester Rosichan, a dapper little man of seventy-two who danced with the Lady when she was in her twenties and he in his thirties, during the war years, when music was the last refuge of festivity. I'm speaking metaphorically, of course, because Lester didn't actually dance *with* the hotel but in it, far into the hours of the morning.

I don't know what the "A" in his name stands for because he wouldn't say, but he did say he was in an Army artillery unit stationed nearby from 1942 to 1946 and the Ambassador was his headquarters.

Lester was making his way down the hotel's main corridor when I saw him. He wore slacks, a yellow leather jacket and a Greek fisherman's cap cocked rakishly on his head. The walk was slow, almost laborious, assisted by a cane. Several strokes had slowed his pace. There would be no dancing till dawn for Lester anymore.

"The memories this place holds," he said, when I asked what had brought him out on this rainy day. "I used to come here

103

maybe three or four times a week for dinner or a drink and then dancing." He hesitated for a moment, remembering, and then said with the satisfaction of one who has touched elusive feathers of the past, "I drank Glenlivet Scotch in those days."

He met his wife thirty-nine years ago not far from the hotel on Berendo Street where they both had apartments. They dated in the Cocoanut Grove. "We had such good times," Lester said. "I wanted to buy a trinket or something today to help me remember. Not anything expensive, a small thing, but the store was closed." He looked around and shook his head. "Well, that's it, I guess."

I watched him shuffle slowly down the corridor past Taffy's and the London Shop and tried to re-create what Lester had been and what the Lady had been when the music played and the dancers whirled and we thought the party would never end.

Then I left too and went to those fire-black homes in the Valley and stood in the softly falling rain, thinking about caprice, an Old Lady dying and about A. Lester Rosichan walking painfully down that corridor of time.

A FANTASY NAMED ANGELYNE

There is a sad, desperate quality to the woman who calls herself Angelyne, like a clown still performing long after the circus has closed.

I say this despite the playful manner in which she displays herself as a Hollywood sex kitten with a Betty Boop cant, flouncing down the street in a zebra-striped minidress with a decolletage that borders on burlesque.

She becomes a caricature, rather than a real person, as tenuous as the murals and billboards she buys all over town to create her own fame.

"I am," she once remarked, "famous for doing nothing."

To see her in person and talk to her at length is to see and talk to someone who, through whatever means available, has achieved the status of *character*—always intriguing but rarely compelling.

One is drawn by the audacity of an orphan girl from the Potato State to be the Angelyne she has contrived on her own, but at the same time made uneasy by the excessive nature of the creation.

"Did you see that?" men say as she passes. They stare at her aberrant, hip-swinging presence much longer than they would at most women, but more in incredulity than admiration.

They scan the implausible zebra dress, the wildly-bouffant blond hair, the excessive fuchsia makeup and the manner in which she presents her ample bust line the way one watches a parade go by.

There's noise and color, but what's the point?

It should be painfully apparent to anyone who sees my work that I like characters, and the town is full of them.

They hang by their ankles from tall buildings, form kazoo bands, dress in chicken costumes and jump up and down half-naked on street corners shouting, "Look at me, look at me!"

Any big city attracts them, but L.A. especially, because they want to be in show biz, and this is where show biz is.

Angelyne, therefore, is a perfect metaphor for those who strive with limited talent and staggering ingenuity to be seen.

But she's too bright, in that intuitive way merchants are bright, to simply sing her song on a street corner.

Angelyne has sold pieces of her career to finance murals and billboards that present her puckered-lip, baby doll face to the world with a single name in glaring pink letters. *Angelyne.*

It all began almost ten years ago, and since then she has become a kind of icon of silly Hollywood, wearing outfits too preposterous to be enticing for a persona too obvious to be ignored.

She boasts two hundred and fifty media conquests (two hundred and fifty-one now, I guess), both print and electronic, and has appeared as herself in five movies in, as one director describes it, "lean-in parts."

Her latest is a short scene in a Steve Martin film, *L.A. Story.*

"I play a famous person in a posh restaurant," she says. "There's an earthquake and my chest starts shaking"—she demonstrates—"but I don't notice. I just keep talking as though nothing has happened."

She sees the quizzical expression on my face and says, "It's OK to make fun of my chest."

We met at Larry Parker's twenty-four-hour Beverly Hills Diner, where so many of L.A.'s characters gather, hoping to have their names affixed to an item on Parker's extensive menu.

Angelyne is both No. seven hundred and twenty-one, the grilled whitefish, and No. four hundred and fifty-five, the broiled hamburger patty. I don't know why. Neither does she.

Much is unknown about this self-styled "love goddess," including her age. It's somewhere over thirty. When I ask why she calls herself a love goddess, she replies, "Because I love God," and giggles.

Angelyne claims to be from Idaho. She says she was raised by foster parents after her own mother and father died.

"Maybe," she says when I ask, "that's why I want attention. No one gave it to me when I was a child."

Perfect. The waif from a nowhere place, orphaned in childhood, struggling to make it on the streets of a town too tough to cry. Who cares if it's true? It's Hollywood.

Angelyne (she won't give her true name) was a beauty queen in high school and, though a self-proclaimed prude, sees nothing evil in the garish physiology of her creation.

"The Bible says when feminine aspects come to light, it will be a better world," she explains in a voice that manages to be alternately squeaky and whispery. "Well, maybe not the Bible, but I read it somewhere."

What next? She's writing a movie about a movie that opens with Angelyne placing her bust prints in pink cement.

But that's only a means to an end. Someday she'd like to play Juliet and make enough money to build her own laboratory.

As we part, she says, "I've always wanted to be a genetic scientist. Well, ta-ta."

Right.

BETTE AND MICHAEL

Promises made in high school are like leaves in an autumn wind, soon flung to the distance and forgotten in an evolution of seasons that creates new priorities.

Gone the quickest, tumbling toward the horizon, are those graduation-day vows that swear eternal love and friendship, and promise that a link formed in pubescence will last forever.

Youthful passions cool quickly, friends pursue widely different goals, and gaps between them widen into chasms.

Old promises, like old leaves, litter a landscape beyond memory, and the winds of change rarely blow them back into our lives.

There are, of course, exceptions, and I sing today of a friendship so sweet and rare it assumes a life of its own, and places in perspective the caprice of unions forged with lesser ties.

This is a song of Bette and Michael.

She couldn't see him, and he couldn't love her, but their friendship based on a promise made in high school by a gay man to a blind woman endured until the day he died.

Bette Ozburn, now thirty-two, has not had an easy life. Cancer blinded her in infancy, a heart seizure almost killed her and a mental breakdown plunged her into a darkness of the soul even deeper than the darkness she faces every day of her life.

But there has always been Michael at her side during the

most difficult times, to hold her hand, to take her arm, to talk with her, and sometimes just to be next to her in silence.

He taught her to laugh, and he taught her to be strong.

His last name was Martinez. We weren't related, though I would have liked that. Michael was the kind of guy who put money in the parking meters of strangers and rushed from Glendale to San Francisco on his own after the earthquake to help save lives.

"He had a strength that never faltered," Bette said the other day in her tiny Burbank apartment. She is a small, pretty woman with a smile that flickers like sunlight through the trees.

"He was gruff on the outside, but gentle on the inside. I knew when I was with Michael, nothing would ever happen to me."

They met as sophomores at Hoover High School in Glendale. At first, she rejected his friendship. Bette was shy and frightened and didn't want pity. But Michael persisted. Pity wasn't what he was offering.

"He was different," she said. "Most people shy away from the blind. Michael would come to the school's blind center. He encouraged me and never treated me as someone different. He believed anything was possible in life, despite disabilities."

Bette's feeling toward Michael blossomed into love, but he told her somehow—she can't remember how—that physical love between them was simply not possible. Michael was gay.

This was a friendship not only beyond sight, but beyond the usual passions that bind men and women. This was different. This was love in the purest form it ever takes.

The promise of friendship was made on graduation day. Bette was going away to college. It was her first time away from home.

"I remember we were signing yearbooks when it suddenly hit me," she said. "I ran from the room crying. I was terrified."

Michael followed and put his arms around her. She was afraid that after graduation, he would be gone from her life forever.

"He said to me," Bette remembered, " 'I'll never not be your friend. I promise you that. I'll always be there when you need me.' And he always was."

109

He was there when Bette's fiance died and he was there through the emotional turmoil that followed. He was there for her heart attack, coaxing her back, and he was there as a voice on the telephone when her nights were unbearable.

"He would call from a construction job in Texas," she said, "or an oil rigging job in Louisiana. We'd talk two or three times a day. He brought me strength."

He brought her memories as well, of walks through the park, of concerts under the stars, of Diana Ross singing "Reach Out and Touch," and walking through the audience, and touching them.

Then as quickly as he entered her life, Michael left it.

He died last month in an automobile accident near Ontario. Bette endures the grief with as much equanimity as she can. The tears have all been cried. She busies herself studying psychology in school and sees a therapist regularly.

"The friend who was always there isn't there anymore," she said, "but our friendship will always have meaning. Michael gave me something special."

And he defined for us all the context of a promise that survived time and the deep winters.

He kept it until the very end.

MOSES ON THE BEACH

You remember Malibu Joe. He was the darling old man reeking of pork grease and urine who Malibu took to its heart as its very own Homeless Person. They fed him grapes and Fritos and challenged the world to say Malibu didn't care about the poor.

Joe lived in a clump of oleanders behind a gas station and was seen to ride a battered old bike around town, trying to remember what his name was and why he was pedaling a battered old bike around town.

I referred to him in a column once as a bum because that's what he seemed to be. I was swamped by telephone callers and letter writers who said he was a dear homeless person and I was pond scum.

Malibu felt so strongly about Joe that when he died last year at age ninety-six its citizens erected a plaque in his honor and no doubt remember him fondly over cocktails at the Beaurivage.

I mention him today because if the people of Malibu *really* loved Joe they are going to have a lot more to love if actor Martin Sheen has his way.

Imagine, for instance, a tent city on the beach loaded with lovable Joes.

You know by now, of course, that Sheen was named honorary mayor of Malibu, replacing actress Ali MacGraw, whose essential contribution to the welfare of her community was to look good and talk sweet.

When the Chamber of Commerce recently appointed Sheen to succeed MacGraw, it no doubt expected a ceremonial administration with a similar tilt. Sheen is also cute and has a kind of soft-spoken sweetness to him.

What the chamber apparently forgot, however, is that Sheen, née Estevez, is also something of a social activist who has been arrested a few times in pursuit of peace, clean air and a full belly, all of which Malibu says it's for.

The difference is that Sheen means it, and as proof began his tenure as honorary mayor by declaring Malibu a nuclear-free zone and a sanctuary for the homeless. Not since roof rats were discovered in the Colony has there been such a stunned silence on the beach.

Creating a nuclear-free zone means very little. To the best of my knowledge, there are no proposals to build either nuclear power plants or Minuteman missile silos anywhere near Alice's Restaurant. In the event of war, Malibu will not fire first.

But welcoming the homeless to its canyons and beaches is something else. If God had intended them to live in Malibu, he'd have made them television producers.

I spoke with several Malibuians about it. One compared Sheen to a slightly skewed Moses, standing on a sand dune summoning the masses to follow him to salvation.

"If he feels that strongly about the poor," the person said, "let him open his house at Point Dume to them."

Another characterized Sheen's inaugural address as his first dive off the Malibu springboard and added, "Too bad there wasn't any water in the pool."

Just about everyone thought the actor made a fool of himself. The Chamber of Commerce, which is more concerned with business than social morality, is appalled at the idea of homeless families massing in Malibu.

They reason quite properly that people scratching for beans and blankets are not likely to spend a lot of money buying bikinis or dining on *ecrevisse de mer* at trendy seaside bistros. Their contribution to the economy would be, at best, minimal.

Malibu isn't the only community to view poverty in the abstract. Two years ago, the Los Angeles City Council bought more than one hundred trailers to house the homeless, but have managed to place only sixty-six of them because of neighborhood protests.

Everyone loves the dispossessed, but from a distance.

I agree with Sheen's motives and admire him for having the temerity to offer Malibu as a sanctuary for the poor. Herding the homeless to Hooverville-on-the-beach is a swell idea and possibly a two-hour movie of the week.

I see Sheen as a good-hearted mayor with an egalitarian cant who is eventually run out of town by those who prefer the old way of helping the poor, when they only had to send checks.

Once rid of Sheen and his lopsided concepts of altruism, the town will reassemble the homeless and march them off to a pleasant reservation in the desert where they will be allowed to retain their rich cultural tradition of eating garbage and sleeping in cardboard boxes generously donated by Malibu.

Back on the beach, Ali MacGraw will be named the queen of sweetness on a platform of smiling prettily and saying nice things. Her first official act will be to canonize Malibu Joe, whose image will miraculously appear on the fiberglass surface of a six hundred dollar high-performance Natural Progression surfboard.

Oh, the hosannas. Oh, the joy. Hold on the happiness, freeze frame and fade out.

ADIOS, MI FERNANDO

Ever since the Dodgers bounced Fernando Valenzuela, I have been overwhelmed by people saying I ought to go to bat, so to speak, for my fellow countryman.

Letters demand I take a stand and telephone callers challenge me to be heard. Not all of them are Mexicans.

One caller was a man named Gottlieb who said if a Jew had been as unceremoniously canned as Fernando, he would certainly do something about it.

"What would you do?" I asked.

"I'd never go to another Dodgers game," he said righteously.

"I don't go to Dodgers games anyhow," I said. "I don't have time to watch grown men hit a ball with a stick."

"Well," Gottlieb replied, "you at least ought to have compassion for a fellow . . . er . . ."

He paused, uncertain whether to refer to me as Latino, Hispanic, Mexican-American, Chicano or Chorizo.

"For a fellow what?" I said, pressing.

"For a fellow brown person!" he said. Then he hung up.

"He called me a brown person," I said to my wife, who had been listening.

"I see you more as burnt umber," she said.

Though a nonprotester, she was also upset when Fernando got *el booto*.

"Another Mexican bites the dust," was the way she put it.

"He bit the dust with several million pesos in his pocket," I said.

"I could use a Mexican with that kind of earning power," she said. "You don't get rich taking up with a drive-by poet."

Members of the brown community are enraged over Fernando's un-mounding.

Leaders of the Mexican-American Political Association and the League of United Latin American Citizens, who know a high-profile protest when they see one, are calling for a boycott of Dodgers games.

They accuse the team's management of not liking Mexicans, or at least of liking Puerto Ricans better. I don't see how that's possible, but to each his own minority.

I spoke with one of the baseball activists who said that firing Fernando was a slap in the face of L.A.'s entire Mexican population.

She's a *gringa* with time on her hands who has taken us brown people to her wrinkled bosom.

"How would blacks like it if the Chicago Bulls fired Michael Jordan?" she demanded.

"If he had lost his ability to slam-dunk," I said, "I think they'd understand."

"The Dodgers haven't heard the last of this," she said. *"Adios!"*

Click.

I don't know a lot of Mexicans, except for the woman who cleans our house once a week. She's never heard of Fernando and doesn't *comprendo* baseball.

However, I did talk to a half-dozen people outside a restaurant on the Eastside. Not one felt as though the Dodgers had toppled a saint.

"He can't pitch anymore," one man said. "What's the team supposed to do, stuff and mount him?"

A woman named Ventura Sedana said she would light a candle for him.

"He isn't dead," I said.

"That's a blessing," she replied.

There are some ethnic causes I have supported wholeheartedly.

I didn't eat table grapes when Cesar Chavez said not to. I'm not sure why I wasn't supposed to eat them. There are some things you accept on faith.

Also, I boycotted Fritos until they got rid of the stereotypical Frito Bandito. That's not exactly the moral equivalent of putting my life on the line for *la raza,* but you get the idea.

So maybe I'm not as ethnic as I ought to be, but I'm not going to fall to my knees sobbing over the unfrocking of a baseball pitcher who happens to be Mexican.

Sure, I understand the need for role models.

I speak occasionally to schools in brown-skinned areas so the kids may see to what heights an umber person can rise in a nation run by whitebreads.

I try to show up on time, sober and with my fly zippered in order to present as decent a picture as possible of a man who has made it out of the lettuce fields.

I doubt that I am perceived as a hero, but if they want to follow my example, *vaya con dios,* baby. Just don't go to pieces if I'm replaced someday by a Lithuanian.

There are many things worth protesting. Spitting in school. Swearing in church. Showing up naked at a funeral. But marching into hell for a pitcher who can't pitch anymore just ain't worth the bloodshed.

The protest proves this much, however. You don't fire a Mexican in this town and get away with it. I sleep better just knowing that.

MAKE IT ONE FOR MY BABY

The cabaret was dark when saloon singer Nick Edenetti stepped to the microphone and waited for the spot to hit him. Moments before, he'd been introduced with a blast from the Nick Fryman Trio. The house lights were out. Only candles flickered on the white-topped tables.

But no spot stabbed through the shadows.

"Nick," a voice finally said from somewhere in the darkness, "can you come here for a minute?"

You could barely see Edenetti's face by candlelight. He seemed confused.

"What'd you mean 'come here?' I'm doing a show."

"The spot doesn't work," the voice said. "I think the light is burned out."

"Then get another light, for God's sake. I'm up here ready to sing."

They raised the house lights a little so you could at least get a better look at Nick. The voice in the dark left to get another spotlight somewhere.

Nick made the best of it. He was already at the mike, so he'd sing in the shadows. He opened with "All of Me," and the show was on.

We were at Gio's restaurant and cabaret in Hollywood. There were maybe fifteen people in the room at the time, only part of whom were listening to Nick. The others were ordering drinks or just talking.

It was just like being at a restaurant in Burbank called the China Den, where Nick got only slightly more attention than the Szechwan pork.

I met him there a year ago and when I heard he was singing at Gio's. I had to see if things had gotten any better for him. Not much.

The waitress passed back and forth in front of him as though he wasn't there, which, I suppose, is what she had to do. Through it all, Nick just kept singing, like he was playing the Met or something.

I mean, not for a moment did he give it less than everything he had, whatever talent, experience and enthusiasm he could dredge up from years on the road, playing little towns and noisy clubs, when lights didn't work and mikes went dead and a lot worse things happen.

"You get used to it," he said later, after the voice in the dark had gotten a new light and they'd figured out which filter looked best on Nick, with people in the audience shouting suggestions.

"Things go wrong sometimes, but that's OK. You figure they've got to get better tomorrow."

Meanwhile, though, before the new light came, he moved in and out of the shadows as the audience grew and chairs scraped and people settled down and the waitress took drink orders.

He sang about rainy days and lost laughter, and when the song was over he looked out into the darkness and said, "You may not be many, but you definitely are few." I think somebody laughed. Maybe not.

When Nick was at Burbank's China Den he was doing a kind of impersonation of Frank Sinatra. A "playography."

Nick works hard at sounding like Sinatra and, in the right kind of light, you'd swear it was old Blue Eyes himself up there on the stool giving you "Night and Day." Belting out "Chicago."

118

I hadn't heard from Nick for more than a year after China Den. Then one night I got home about two A.M. and turned on the television to relax, and there was Edenetti on the screen with a group of comics I have never heard of.

The station was KSCI-TV, which I also had never heard of. Nick was acting as host, and, during a break for commercials, they announced that it was the Nick Edenetti All Night Show, from one to six every Sunday morning.

So I looked Nick up and, sure enough, he was into the ninth week of being a kind of poor man's Johnny Carson, buying the air time himself, gambling that he'll make it, the way he's always gambled doing clubs.

"I've got Steve Allen and Barbara Eden coming next week," he said that night at Gio's between acts. "You remember her from 'I Dream of Jeannie'? Then Ann Miller and some other people."

James Bacon, an old-time Hollywood columnist, is Nick's sidekick on the show, which is mixed talk and variety. Nick calls him Jim McBacon. Like Ed McMahon. Get it?

At Gio's, Nick was complaining he'd been off the air for two weeks because of technical difficulties. It was never made clear what these difficulties were, but they were serious enough to cause five hours of test patterns in place of his show.

"We'll be back," Nick said. "Count on it."

I have no doubt. There is a tenacity about Edenetti you don't find in many people. An honesty, too. He's a saloon singer, and he's proud of it.

No castles in the air. No smoke in the spotlight. He's what he is. Period.

I thought about that when he was singing in the dark, moving against a row of dim lights that lined a back wall, a silhouette with a mike doing "I've Got the World on a String."

I thought about it as chairs scraped and people talked and the cocktail waitress said, "On the rocks or straight up?" and as Nick went into "I've Got You Under My Skin."

There's something about the guy I admire. Something about

singing in the dark and singing in the noise. Something about always trying, no matter what.

When the spot came on for the first time, Nick spread his arms and smiled and bowed like he'd been singing for the Queen.

He got a nice hand.

TEARS IN A PALE APARTMENT

If you were looking for symbols, Easter was a glorious day of rebirth. Sunlight scattered gold on the ocean and emeralds on the hillsides, turning L.A. into a gleaming panorama of high color and clean air.

That's what Easter is supposed to be, a surge of renewal from the darkness of winter, a resurrection of the spirit on a day as bright as heaven.

I saw Easter in children dancing on a morning lawn, the ebullience of their youth captured in a blur of laughter, their dance an unstructured gift to spring.

Their names are Nicole, Shana and Travis.

The ritual of egg-hunting over, they had become swept up in a rhythm only the young can hear, leaping and whirling gazelle-like under a canopy of glowing blue.

Their laughter was as clean as wind chimes in a sudden breeze.

I see them even now as clouds gather on a Monday morning, their heads thrown back and their arms outstretched, calling on me to watch as they move to the music in their heads.

The memory is a sustaining one . . . but darker thoughts intrude.

Life, I keep remembering, is not all children dancing on the lawn or sunlight on green hillsides. Tears too often streak the face of the city I write about.

There is sorrow, guilt and loneliness in this population bowl of nine million, and no one knows that better than a journalist.

Consider the case of Carolyn Lappin, who weeps for the past.

She telephoned one day to say she couldn't stop grieving for a mother who died eight years ago. Guilt and loneliness were eating her alive.

"It isn't just that," she said. "Nothing is the same anymore. Movies are different. The world is changing without me in it."

Her mother had been a close companion, but when she was dying of emphysema, Carolyn, now in her forties, couldn't stand the thought of her death and ran from her.

"I didn't even say good-bye," she said that day over the telephone. "And now"—her voice broke—"I can't stop crying."

I can't be everyone's therapist. I'm not going to sponge up everyone's grief. But there was something compelling here.

Carolyn became a metaphor for a woman I once saw crying at a bus stop, and for a man with tears in his eyes watching boys play baseball in a park.

They were people in grief I didn't write about but can't forget. Through Carolyn, my own atonement seemed at hand.

I stopped by to hear her story, and in a way I wish I hadn't. Sorrow has a way of embracing all within reach.

Her small apartment overlooking Santa Monica Bay is a study in flat white: white sofas, white carpets, white walls, white lampshades. Large mirrors double the whiteness and create an illusion of disquieting emptiness.

With light hair and pale skin, Carolyn Lappin is an integral part of that bleak and lonely motif.

Once an aspiring actress ("I always wanted to be someone else"), she gave it up when a relationship with a man fell apart and she moved in with her mother.

When her mother died, everything fell apart.

"She had become my whole life," Carolyn says, sitting by a window that looks north toward the Santa Monica Mountains. Anguish lines her face.

"Without my boyfriend and my mother, I feel an over-whelming loneliness. There is no one to know where I am, or

122

where I've been. I could drive forever and who would care?"

Carolyn recalls with vivid clarity the day her mother told her of her illness.

"A Santa Ana was blowing," she says. "The sky was pale. It was quiet and very strange . . ."

They had done everything together. They had cooked together, walked on the beach together, traveled together and confided in each other.

But when her mother fell ill, Carolyn couldn't take it. She refused requests even to visit her in the hospital.

She doesn't know why. A psychotherapist, Michael Aharoni, says she was a witness to her own mortality, and it terrified her.

Her mother was in a coma the last six months of her life. Crushed by guilt, Carolyn finally rushed to her side.

"I begged her forgiveness," she says, "but I don't even know if she heard me. Now she's gone and never coming back."

"What do you want of me?" I asked.

"Just mention her name," Carolyn said. "Just put her in your column."

If recognition can lessen grief and quiet the hounds of guilt, so be it. Her name was Nettie Lappin.

Now, perhaps, Carolyn can get back to living, and I can relax on a day dark with rain clouds and remember three small children dancing in the golden sunlight of Easter.

TEARS ON THE PAVEMENT

I bummed around Sylmar in the hours past midnight last week, like a cat prowling dark alleys, sniffing out whatever I could find. It was on a Thursday and there was a quarter moon.

I do that sometimes when I can't sleep. Trivial anxieties become mind-chewing monsters in the psychedelic madness of insomnia, and it's better to run than fight.

So I get in the car and wander.

L.A. is always awake anyhow. Freeways hum with traffic, markets and laundromats go all night, tennis courts stay open and twenty-four-hour restaurants are almost always busy.

My angry old stepfather, who also never slept, used to go out in the yard in his underwear at night and dig in the garden, no matter what time it was.

"It was the Great Depression," my mother explained one day, when I asked why he did that.

She blamed everything on the Depression, no matter what, and while I never did quite understand why it made him garden by moonlight in his shorts, I didn't pursue it.

I was fully dressed the night I ended up at Denny's, just off the Golden State Freeway at the foot of the Roxford Street off-ramp.

I was having a cup of coffee at the counter, studying the tattoos of an old guy about three seats away, when a woman sat deliberately next to him and struck up a conversation.

It was The Night Harry Met Sally.

At first I didn't pay much attention but then she said, "Do you come here often?" I couldn't believe I'd heard that.

It was like she was a dark-eyed beauty at some swinging singles bar trying to score with a Sagittarian.

But this was Denny's, not T.G.I. Friday's, and Sally was no dark-eyed beauty. She was maybe on the dumpy downside of thirty-five and had skin like the face of the moon.

Her hair hung in tangled bunches and looked like it hadn't been washed in a long time. She had teeth missing.

Harry was no great catch either. He was maybe seventy-plus, wrinkled, balding and wore a scowl like the fires of hell were burning in his gut.

He reminded me of my stepfather, whose name was Harry, and who had naked-women tattoos up and down both arms. That's why the name of that movie, *When Harry Met Sally* . . . popped into my head.

But trust me when I say this was no encounter between Meg Ryan and Billy Crystal.

Harry slurped his coffee like a dog drinking from a bowl and hardly looked up when Sally talked. He was reading a *National Enquirer* and grumbled in response every once in a while.

The place was noisy so I couldn't hear everything Sally said and I couldn't hear Harry at all. Truckers, bikers and retired people traveling in motor homes came and went, and surly young guys who looked furtive and predatory.

A woman sat by herself in a corner drinking black coffee and smoking cigarettes, staring out at the night. Her eyes glistened in the flashing headlights of passing traffic, and I wondered if she were crying.

I had kind of drifted away from any interest in Harry and Sally, but then I heard Sally's voice in a metered cadence and glanced over to see what she was up to.

Damned if she wasn't reading poetry from a scrap of paper. Harry had even put down the *National Enquirer* and was listening.

Pieces of the poem fell through the noise like leaves in winter, and I only got a word or a phrase here and there.

There was something about a child crying and "small gasps of desperation."

Small gasps of desperation. . . .

Had Sally written that? She didn't look like a poet, but then how does a poet look? Art is where you find it.

I once heard a junkie describe the long, dark halls of his addiction in a poetry of pain that wrenched the soul. I heard a guy with a guitar playing music in a tunnel that haunts me to this day like a half-remembered dream.

Why not art in Denny's?

Sally finished reading the poem and Harry just stared at her for a moment, the way a lion stares at an antelope when he isn't hungry, without interest or passion.

I heard her say something about a place to stay. Harry mumbled in reply, put money on the counter and got up and left without looking back.

Sally had given it everything she had but Harry wasn't buying. In a moment or two, she was gone too, and so was the woman at the window with tears in her eyes and the couple with the motor home.

I kept thinking I was a lot like Sally, trading words for a place to stay, only luckier.

I finished my coffee and headed for home. *Small gasps of desperation.* Not bad. Not bad at all. She should've been paid.

BEAUTY AND THE BEASTIE

There is something about seventy-one beauty contestants in one place that has a numbing effect on the brain. They tend to blur into a single entity after a while, with one brilliant smile, one dazzling hairdo, one cute behind and one proud bust line.

Watching them, an observer is inclined to fantasize they are, indeed, one person, sharing the same age, the same goals, the same interests and the same desires.

They are nineteen, measure 34-24-35, plan on a career in modeling and/or neurosurgery, are serious students of facial aerobics, and number Mikhail Gorbachev, Bon Jovi, Mother Teresa and Brooke Shields among those they most admire.

Put them all in a jar, add water, shake vigorously and, *voila,* Miss Universe 1990. Applause, hugs, brave smiles, tears, cash awards, fade out.

So.

As you might suspect, I stopped by the Century Plaza Hotel one day to observe a preliminary activity for the Miss Universe Contest, which was to be televised on CBS.

Those who relied solely on the fast-format, easy-readin' L.A. *Times* for their information were perhaps not aware the pageant was even taking place. We had not covered it with what is known in the trade as a *real* reporter.

They sent me instead.

I happened by on Swimsuit Day, during which all the "delegates," as they are known, paraded in their bikinis before at least an equal number of photographers and then settled into a single cluster for additional picture-taking.

I was, of course, appalled by the sexist nature of the event in this era of gender neutrality and left immediately after the last pert tush had vanished behind closed doors.

While I was there, however, I was impressed by the clockwork efficiency of the colloquium, which, by the way, concluded with the selection of Miss Photogenic. I don't know who won, but does it matter?

Statistics for the composite beauty contestant mentioned earlier were furnished by the pageant's public relations team, although I admit to embellishing them for, as we way, satirical purposes.

Truth is not a serious factor when you're covering a beauty pageant. Let the good times roll.

I was even supplied with a list of questions I might like to ask, including but not limited to, "Can delegates be married?" "Are delegates allowed to have cosmetic surgery?" and "Are delegates required to have a coach?"

Thank God, the answers also were furnished (no, yes, no), thus sparing me the necessity of doing anything but evaluating the relentlessly smiling delegates, some of whom had obviously challenged the limits of their abilities by also learning to cock their heads.

Simultaneously smiling and cocking one's head is no small accomplishment among those who aspire to beauty-hood, requiring as it does an almost instinctive ability to gauge angle and tilt factor with rigid coordination.

It should not be tried at home by amateurs.

The delegate from Argentina, a green-eyed beauty named Paola Torre, led the alphabetically arranged parade of nations past photographers who had come to L.A. from as far away as Turkey specifically to emulsify this event.

There is something about a photographer, no matter where he's from, that brands him by trade, much as a pentagram in the palm identifies a werewolf.

I was especially impressed with the universal nature of a cameraman's ability to communicate complex requests in simple terms. One, for instance, shouted "Hey, Korea" to indicate he wanted Miss Korea to pose for him.

Over the years, I have also heard them shout "Hey, Pope," meaning the holy pontiff, and "Hey, Queen," meaning her majesty, Queen Elizabeth II.

In heaven, should one ever get there, I have no doubt he would shout, "Hey, God!"

The only moment of distress in the morning's proceedings came when Miss England, a beauty therapist (whatever that is) from Nottingham, appeared to have fainted.

For a moment, I thought she had simply over-cocked her head and fallen off the bench.

It was explained later, however, that Carla Barrow, who lists "eating out" among her hobbies, had failed to eat breakfast that day, a mistake somehow leading to her momentary swoon.

Even the keeling-over of Miss England, however, was handled with discreet good taste by pageant officials, who are no doubt trained for just such an emergency. Miss E. appeared later, her equanimity intact.

I was, in fact, impressed generally with the ability of the girls, I mean delegates, to strut their saucy stuff under such trying circumstances.

It can't be easy maintaining your composure when everyone is staring at your erogenous zones.

A FUN LITTLE RICE CRACKER

I was sitting around the other day discussing triglycerides and complex carbohydrates with my wife when it occurred to me that chamomile tea would probably never replace the simple martini.

The reason we were on the subject is that I have undertaken a special diet which, it is said, may add ten years to my life. I am not sure, however, it will be the kind of life worth living.

I have entered the program not to join the parade of skinny old men shuffling through L.A., clinging to life by a thread as tenuous as a strand of linguini, but to get my heart back into the shape it ought to be.

There is nothing like the fear of death to draw one's attention to good nutrition. So follow along as we witness the pathetic descent of a lusty gourmand into the gray world of plain gelatin and buckwheat flour.

The diet basically reduces to a minimum fats and cholesterol-causing foods at my table. Should a cow accidentally wander into the kitchen, I am to kill it instantly and burn the carcass.

Cows in any form, to hear my dietician tell it, are a part of my past.

A typical dinner menu under the prevailing stringent conditions, for instance, will allow me the following for a lip-smacking meal:

One-half cup of skim milk, three small servings of vegetables, one small apple, one ear of corn and 3.5 ounces of fish.

If I am still hungry after that, as surely I will be, I may indulge in "a fun little rice cracker" for nutrition and, I suppose, for laughs.

I have managed to avoid that so far, sparing myself fun with a rice cracker until a more desperate time.

My metabolism, meanwhile, is fueled by a precise blend of proteins, complex carbohydrates, fruits, vegetables and fat-free dairy products in such fine balance that I am afraid to tamper with it.

I don't know what would happen, for instance, if I had two complex carbohydrates and no fruit at one meal. I might explode.

The possibility is haunting. The other day I was about to sit down to a bowl of delicious cardboard-flavored vegetarian chili and lima beans cooked in rain water when I suddenly began to wonder, God help me, if my chili was clashing with my lima beans.

It's sad to see a grown man accustomed to the hearty enjoyment of *poitrine de veau* abruptly in a panic over his vegetarian chili, but there I was, going down a list of food-exchanges on a card from my pocket to see if the nutritional balance was proper.

"Easy," my wife said, when she noticed I was beginning to perspire.

"Easy, hell," I said. "I may be creating deadly chemistry in my body by mixing chili and lima beans."

"You're overreacting to a simple program of nutrition."

"There is nothing simple about this diet," I said. "I am supposed to have green sapsago cheese and no sorbitol or manitol." I leaned closer. "I don't even know what the hell sorbitol and manitol are."

"Poor dear," she said.

I have committed myself to this Spartan existence for a month and have pretty much abided by the unforgiving menu, with the possible exception of last night when I said to hell with my triglycerides and drank a dry vodka martini. Well, actually, two. And I didn't feel a damned bit guilty about it.

My poor attitude strikes at the very core of the program.

131

I was warned at its outset that the most important part of the regimen was a positive mental approach.

"That," my wife said later, "is going to be your Achilles' heel."

Possibly. For example, I am emotionally incapable of carrying a can of unsweetened baby food or a "grain beverage," whatever the hell that is, to a restaurant in order to maintain my program of good nutrition while dining out.

I am further incapable of "speaking up with appropriate restaurant suggestions when in a group," insofar as those suggestions might encompass a cheerful call for cooked Wheatena or another round of unsalted eggplant.

I'd rather eat dog than eat eggplant.

However, I do understand the importance of good food at this faltering stage in my life, so a plate of Chinese cabbage, cooked celery and unflavored broccoli will do me no harm, though I must remember to go easy on foods containing oxalic acids.

There is no point in a healthy heart if I O.D. on beet greens.

Nevertheless, I have, as I mentioned, remained reasonably true to my health program with that one slippage into the ugly swamp of vodka and vermouth.

We were in the bar at Tail O' the Cock.

"You're ordering a martini?" my wife asked, surprised.

"Right," I said. "But, and this is important, *no olive*. The olives are deadly."

"Booze is deadly."

"All right," I said, "I'll have a martini, you have chamomile tea."

She thought about that for a moment and then said, "One margarita, with salt, hold the straw."

We had such a hell of a good time, we skipped the rice crackers.

WELCOME TO THE WAR

I am sitting in a hot little upstairs room in Santa Monica, surrounded by television cameras and listening to an attractive young woman talk about how to guard the doors when the war starts.

"You link arms," Robin Schneider says, "and you line up in three rows in this manner."

She demonstrates to the assembled reporters by placing maybe a dozen trainees near the door to the room and showing them where to stand.

"The reason you face in different directions," she explains, "is if their people try to crawl through, they can't."

Next she uses the trainees to demonstrate an escort strategy, moving someone from here to there safely. Arms are linked again. Words like "combat" and "skirmish" creep into her language.

Strobe lights pop. Television cameras hum. On-camera news personalities nod authoritatively, the way they've been taught to do when they're still trying to figure out what's going on.

Schneider is executive director of the California Abortion Rights Action League, under whose auspices this combined press conference and battle demonstration is being held.

"Any questions?" she asks at the end.

It is the first day of spring. There is a faint aroma of Giorgio in the room. The whole thing is surreal.

Talk of war has got me thinking. "Is there a possibility they have spies here?" I ask.

"That's possible," Schneider says, waiting for my follow-up question. I have none. It was a whim of the moment.

I think about asking if anyone will parachute behind enemy lines but dismiss the idea.

"Is it possible you have infiltrated *them?*" I finally ask.

"That's possible," Schneider says.

"Well, well," I say, writing furiously in my mauve notebook and thinking that we never had mauve notebooks in the old days of newspapering.

Welcome to the war.

That day began three days of confrontation during which those who oppose abortions will try to shut down the abortion clinics in Southern California. They'll crawl through the doors if necessary and sit in.

It is also the beginning of a three-day period during which those who favor abortion will try to stop those who oppose abortion from shutting down the clinics in Southern California. They'll link arms and stand firm.

The anti-abortionists call themselves pro-life advocates. The pro-abortionists call themselves pro-choice advocates.

You are either for life or for choice. If you favor choice, you're a whore and a murderer, which are terms employed by the attackers. If you are pro-life, you are a sexist pig and a religious nut, which are terms employed by the defenders.

During the Korean War, I tried to engage a gunnery sergeant in the relative merits of communist ideology. "It don't matter what their merits are," the gunny replied. "Shoot them."

Wars are like that. We don't expect any shooting during what the anti-abortionists call the Holy Week of Rescue. But there will be a kind of cultural violence unleashed upon us all. Hatreds will explode like missiles. Words will wound like bullets.

I talked to a woman earlier this week who couldn't wait to shut down the abortion clinics. "God will prove us right," she said, her voice rising. "He will crush them and bless us!"

"Shoot them," the gunny had said.

"We are here to prepare ourselves for the skirmish this week and to be troops in the battles ahead," Robin Schneider says into a cluster of microphones at the press conference.

Behind her is a large poster: KEEP ABORTION SAFE AND LEGAL. Lady Liberty holds her torch high.

"You are heroes in defense of our civil rights," actress Brynn Thayer says. She's a regular on the series "TV 101." No press conference is complete without a celebrity, however scant and temporary fame might be.

"We are not vigilantes," Schneider says to the trainees. "We do not want to do anything to increase the level of conflict in the three days ahead. Do not wear dangly earrings!"

I write that down, but it occurs to me that I don't know why the defenders of the clinics shouldn't wear dangly earrings. "The pro-lifers grab for them," a pro-choicer explains later. "Necklaces too."

The gunny had said to me, "Write your mother while she's still alive and don't worry about the other side."

Ah, war. Ah, spring. How strange.

DOIN' THE HOT LAMBADA

The place is jumping like a Joe Carioca cartoon.

Miranda Garrison is in the middle of the room, black dress slit to her waist and decolletage down to the legal limit, both arms flung out and pelvis thrust forward, dancing with a kid who is sweating from more than just physical exertion.

She is moving to a pulsating Latin rhythm in a way that contributes to the greenhouse effect and shouting "feel the beat, feel the beat," as maybe eighty others dance or practice in front of a wall of mirrors, their behinds swaying like palm trees in a Santa Ana.

They're doing the lambada.

Well, that is to say, they are attempting to do the lambada, because that's what everyone who is anyone is doing, and we've all got to be up there swaying and thrusting with the rest of them.

Not since the Romans discovered the social nature of an orgy have so many been doing the same thing at the same time in the same room.

Naturally, they were doing it in Hollywood.

Miranda, a choreographer, and Loreen Arbus, a television producer with an unexplainable interest in Latin dances, are offering lessons in the lambada at the Landmark Studio.

I dropped by because public eroticism appeals to my sense of recollected evil, tapping a memory of youth when something called the dirty boogie was an undergound hit.

I never did actually dance it because my mother said that if I did I'd go to hell, but I had a great time watching and shouting, "Hey, man, that's what I crave," which were the words of the song that set us high school studs into a primitive frenzy.

The mere memory makes my palms itch.

Notwithstanding that faint stirring, I became interested in the lambada because, as I said, that's what you all seem to be doing and I don't want you doing anything of which I don't approve. Think of me as a kind of hovering celestial presence.

To prepare for my afternoon of live lambada, I first saw the movie *Lambada, Set the Night on Fire*. Trust me when I say it doesn't.

It is, briefly, the story of a pretty male high school teacher who says things like "Hey, chill out, man," and gets involved with some pretty barrio kids who want to, like, make it in the pretty Anglo world by learning trigonometry.

You see it all the time in the barrio, kids tripping out on trig.

Additional dialogue, for those who favor the art form, includes "You're not the brightest candle on the cake" and "Let 'em duke it out with their brains." Shakespeare couldn't have said it better.

Interwoven through all this for no apparent reason is the dancing of the Brazilian-born lambada, during which enough pelvises are rubbed together and legs entwined to cause smoke, if not fire.

I hear you say wow, that sounds, you know, erotic, but don't be fooled. Sex and vacuity are more feral than sensual, and unless you're turned on by the mating call of a bowhead whale, this movie isn't for you.

In the theater at the time were fourteen teenagers, two old ladies, a male pervert and me. The film was so unappealing that even the pervert left before it was over. I stayed because, well, it's my job.

Meanwhile, back in Hollywood, I am watching Miranda Garrison on the dance floor having more fun than an otter on a mud bank, while the kid she'd dancing with is trying to look cool and not scratch his palms.

137

I realize the juxtaposition of an otter with a dancer is an uncomfortable union of metaphors, but it seems oddly apropos in this case. Use your imagination.

The lambada isn't all sexual, but those aspects of it that are can tingle loins from Miami Beach to Malibu. At one point my wife, who always accompanies me on columns of an erotic nature, looks at me and says, "Close your mouth, you're drooling."

I swear to you I never drool, no matter what. She is using that to illustrate the degree of attention I bring to a project I am researching for future composition.

Neither she nor Miranda see the dance as particularly sexual, though my wife will grant the old Tom Lehrer observation, "When properly viewed, everything's lewd."

"It's the media that makes it sexual," Miranda says as she cools off outside the dance studio. "You'd see more than this at a bar mitzvah. What we interpret as nasty is natural in Brazil, even religious."

Miranda advises me to join in. What she says is, "spread your feet, bend your knees and hang out."

I am tempted, but my wife reminds me that I have a bad back and no sense of rhythm, so I decline.

"It's just as well," she said as we left, "you don't want to end up in hell."

Maybe yes, maybe no.

WHEN THE RUNNING STOPPED

One sees his face through hazy sunshine as the photograph is tilted to ease the glare. Troy Anthony Blocker. The face smiles back at the world with a sweetness as soft as a summer day.

Here is a boy, one thinks, who will run through life with the speed of a gazelle, racing the wind across open fields and down winding pathways, a heartbeat ahead of his past, a half-step behind his future.

And run he did, with an ebullience that only youth can evoke, for Troy was only seven, and seven was a dazzling place to be.

Then one day the running stopped.

Everyone knew it would. Troy had AIDS. Eventually, all that energy, all that sweetness, all that perfect embodiment of life would fade. A rustle in the treetops, then silence.

"Here's another picture," Diane Fink says.

We are sitting at a table in Pan Pacific Park. A basketball is bounced nearby in a steady, drumming rhythm. The laughter of children floats past like petals in a breeze.

"He's with his brother Aaron," she says, shading the picture with her hand. "Aaron was two years younger. When I'd go to their house Aaron would holler, 'Here comes the white lady!'"

Diane smiles.

"They were more than brothers," she says. "They were friends."

Troy Anthony Blocker, April 2, 1981–June 16, 1989.

We meet him vicariously through Diane Fink, a tiny, red-haired woman in her fifties.

Divorced and living comfortably in Beverly Hills, Diane entered Troy's life through the Family Outreach unit of L.A. Youth Programs, an organization that serves children.

Troy had been a premature baby and had contracted AIDS through a blood transfusion. Diane had survived a brain tumor and vowed she would celebrate that survival by helping others.

Their paths crossed last October when Diane was assigned to assist Troy and his family. Soon, she and the brothers were a familiar trio at the Westside's Pan Pacific Park.

"They loved this place," Diane says, looking around. "We came here every Saturday. Regulars would wonder about the white lady and two little black kids. One child came up to me one day and said, 'Do you live together?' "

Troy and Aaron brought their scooters and rode them down the lawn-bordered pathways from an upper play yard to a lower picnic area.

"They would banter back and forth all the way down," Diane says. "You could see the progress of the disease over the weeks. Aaron continued to bloom, but Troy was wilting. . . ."

When he was old enough to understand, Troy was told he had AIDS and would die. He said simply, "Don't tell my friends."

"He was such a bright child," Diane says. "He knew how the fear of the disease creates such a prejudice. Kids with AIDS don't have friends."

She remembers the fifth birthday party of another boy with AIDS.

"Children came to the party but their parents insisted on two cakes. They were afraid the disease would spread when the candles were blown out."

She watches other children play for a moment, then says absently, "In the last weeks, Troy wouldn't look at kids his own age. He'd turn his back as though he couldn't bear to see healthy children. Aaron would ask, 'What's the matter?' but he wouldn't answer."

One of Troy's last great pleasures was a bicycle. He rode it only a few times, until the relentless progress of dying sapped his strength, and he was forced to lean it against the foot of his bed for the last time.

"It was hard for him to ride it," Diane says, "but he kept trying. It was such a brief pleasure. But sometimes a moment's joy is all we get in life, isn't it?"

I came to know Troy that sunny day in the park.

He was everyone's little boy and his death leaves unanswered all the questions of his future, all the glory of his potential. And it also leaves unanswered the last question asked by his brother.

On the morning Troy died, Aaron touched his face and in an anguish that claws at the heart said softly, "I thought we were going to grow up together."

I returned to the park alone the next day and studied Troy's picture. A soft breeze caught it and tilted it toward the sun. His face vanished in the blinding glare.

BARRY'S LONELY AMERICA

I was in a bank the other day depositing a modest few dollars in my Christmas savings account when the teller looked up from her computer, said what sounded like "Wazashee canalonie?" in a thick accent and waited for a reply.

I have no ear for accents. I said, "I beg your pardon?" and she repeated the phrase, "Wazashee canalonie?"

It was obvious from the tilt of her head and the questioning look in her eyes that she expected an answer.

Her finger remained poised over her keyboard. Time stood still.

I could have repeated "Wazashee canalonie" in a bold, declarative manner and let it go at that, hoping it would somehow all work out.

It is a technique I employ when faced with the unknown. But this was a bank, and banks are no place to fool around.

The teller looked Arab. I suspect she was from Kuwait. Maybe her daddy owned a controlling interest in the bank. Maybe he owned Kuwait.

"Look," I said, taking it from the top. "I only want to deposit fifteen dollars in my account."

She seemed confused, so I raised my voice. Foreigners understand better when you shout at them.

"Put the fifteen dollars in," I hollered, "and give me back my deposit book and I'll leave!"

An armed guard at the far end of the bank was beginning

to take notice. Lord help me if he thought I'd said, "Put all the money in a paper bag, and no one will get hurt!"

Shouting Bandit Hits Town. Film at 11.

And all because of an accent. The whole thing reminded me of Barry Hatch.

Hatch is the mayor of suburban Monterey Park. He's been in the news lately because he believes that foreign accents and foreign cultures are ruining America, and he's not going to take it anymore.

He wants to ban immigration into the United States for three years and make English the nation's official language.

These are matters not usually handled out of Monterey Park, but Barry has decided to speak up on the subject for the sake of those Silent Americans who, wisely, remain silent most of the time.

When Barry first began talking about his plan to give America back to the Americans (not the Indians but the more *recent* Americans), he wanted immigration halted for one year.

By the time I reached him, he'd raised the ante to three years.

"We are being colonized by other countries," Hatch said in his Monterey Park office. "Immigration built us, and now it's destroying us."

He is a pink-faced man of fifty-two with thin, graying hair and the manner of a junior high school social studies teacher, which he is. Sometimes he plays tapes of his talk show appearances to his classes.

Barry believes that if Third World people keep coming to America, we will turn into a Third World nation. And because Third World people are have-nots, they will be going for the throats of us haves and it will be adios, peace and quiet.

It would be a better nation with a better future, he hints, if everyone were exactly like . . . well . . . *him.*

My first inclination was to argue that everyone ought to be more like *me,* but then I realized I am one of the little brown people being discussed in the first place, so that wouldn't work out.

It's him or nobody.

Barry speaks in very clear teacher's English so at least there wouldn't be a communications problem if America were limited to people who looked and thought and talked exactly like him.

No bank teller from Kuwait would ask, "Wazashee canalonie?" No elderly Asian lady at Anne's Chinese Deli would ask, "Shunshing?"

Anne's Chinese Deli is in Chatsworth. I ate there for years and always said no to shunshing because I thought it was a sauce made of decaying fish.

Then one say I learned she was saying, "Something?" which was short for "Something to drink?"

Now I know enough to say, "A Diet Pepsi, please," and she says, "Frontang." That means thank you.

Barry wants America's golden doors closed to people like that. Throw up barbed wire. Send the wretched refuse back to their teeming shores.

I have a better idea.

Beat them at their own game, Barry. Migrate.

Find an island or a mountaintop somewhere without a medley of languages, without infringing cultures, without the wretched refuse of those teeming shores.

Build a fence around your own pure enclave, and there you'll achieve what must be the ultimate purpose of your effort anyhow.

You'll discover not that you've locked everyone out, but that you've locked yourself in. In the end that's a lonely place to be.

HEAVY DUTY MOTEL

Mr. Charlie was unhappy.

He stared gloomily at the floor and tried hard to convey the message that this whole business of trying to keep hookers out of his motel was almost too much.

"Some prostitute look like housewife," he was saying, "and some housewife look like prostitute. How you know?"

His friend, Mr. Kuo, nodded in agreement. "Some have driver license!" he added in a proper tone of incredulity.

Mr. Charlie shook his head. "Heavy duty," he said sadly.

We were sitting in a forty dollar room of the Chateau Motel on Sepulveda Boulevard, in what has been described by local merchants as the New Center of Prostitution in the San Fernando Valley.

I don't know what the Old Center was, but that is not essential to the story.

The room was equipped with a water bed, a mirror on the ceiling and a television set over which adult films are offered for those who require . . . well . . . exterior motivation.

Debbie Does Dallas, perhaps. Or the current favorite, *She Wants You.*

There are no telephones in any of the Chateau's forty-four units, Mr. Kuo explained, because customers were stealing so many of them they were all removed.

I believe that's what Mr. Kuo said.

Both Mr. Kuo and Mr. Charlie, which is what they prefer being called, are Chinese, and, while Mr. Charlie does quite well with English, Mr. Kuo does less well.

As a matter of fact, I only understood about thirty percent of what he said, but since I only understood about forty percent of what my mother said for seventy percent of her life, that isn't too bad.

I was at the Chateau to begin with because it was recently named by police as the worst place on the block as far as hookers are concerned.

Or I guess you could say it's the *best* place on the block as far as hookers are concerned, but the worst as far as everyone else is concerned.

In the past year, one hundred and twenty-five arrests have been made at the Chateau, eighty of them involving prostitutes.

This has not pleased the surrounding merchants, especially those who sell gentle, homey items like flowers and doilies and stuffed teddy bears, so they prevailed upon the police to turn up the heat on the hookers.

Well, sir, if there is one thing an L.A. cop understands it is rousting hookers, so they went to Mr. Charlie and told him to clean up or face the consequences.

Which brings us to the forty dollar room with the water bed and the mirror on the ceiling and the closed-circuit TV set, but no phone.

Mr. Charlie manages the Chateau for Mr. Yung, who speaks no English at all. Mr. Kuo, as I understand it, is Mr. Charlie's friend.

I decided to talk with whoever understood anything at the Chateau because too often all the play is given to those in the attack and not always to the attackee.

"Why," I asked Mr. Charlie and Mr. Kuo, "do you allow prostitutes to use your motel?"

Mr. Kuo began to answer but couldn't find the proper English words and handed it over to Mr. Charlie who, Mr. Kuo explained, was educated in Australia. Sydney, I believe.

146

"Don't know who bad," Mr. Charlie said helplessly. "Know eighty percent of prostitute, not twenty percent."

In one instance, Mr. Charlie said, he demanded identification from a woman who, as he saw it, was dressed like a prostitute but who, as it turned out, was the wife of the man accompanying her.

"They both very angry," Mr. Charlie said. "Walk out." He stared forlornly out the window. "Heavy duty," he said.

Mr. Charlie emphasized that he was no friend to hookers. He is going to hire a security guard and raise the height of a surrounding fence in order to keep them out, he said.

Then he showed me a large sign in the lobby of the motel that says NO PROSTITUTES.

There is also a sign that says NO PETS and one that says NO CHECKS and another that sums it all up, NO CHANGE, NO ICE, NO MATCHES.

No kidding.

The Chateau, in addition to a nightly rate, also rents rooms in three-hour increments for twenty-four dollars.

Mr. Charlie has been asked to end the hourly rate, but objects that "regular people" like to rent the rooms for a few hours of fun.

"Nothing wrong with that," he said indignantly.

"Managers bring secretaries here," Mr. Kuo added, grinning.

Mr. Charlie pointed at me. "If you bring secretary here and I ask for I.D., you don't like!"

"I don't have a secretary," I said.

"Too bad," Mr. Charlie said.

I don't know if anyone has a surefire method for recognizing hookers. Not all of them wear red hot pants anymore.

They wear designer jeans and satin jogging suits and sometimes, I guess, simple little print dresses with aprons.

I said to Mr. Charlie, however, that I doubted if many regular housewives would be checking into his motel. Secretaries, maybe, but not housewives.

Mr. Charlie replied that he is being forced to assume every-

147

one is a prostitute and that assumption is causing a decrease in business.

"Even normal people scared to come here," he said.

Mr. Kuo sighed.

"Heavy duty," he said.

SHORT, NOT SWEET

I received a telephone call the other day from a man who said he was sick and tired of my sneering references to short people.

"Fill me in," I said.

"Fill you in on what?"

"On what I said about short people."

"You don't remember what you write?"

"Sometimes. Did I make reference to their nasty little feet?"

"As a matter of fact, yes."

"That sounds like me. And did I say it's tough looking fit when you're short?"

"You sure did."

"I vaguely remember that too. Tell me," I said, "are you short?"

"I am five feet six," he said, "and proud."

"You're proud of being five-six?"

"I am proud," he said, proudly, "of being me."

Under normal circumstances, I would have hung up on Shorty. I rarely debate yesterday's columns, and I do not believe proud, short people have anything important to say.

His call, however, came at a propitious time. Others have communicated with me about my references to short people, especially short men, and I was thinking about exploring the issue in a column devoted exclusively to those of less than heroic stature.

A short column, of course.

One unsigned letter called me a "height-bigot" and said I would no doubt be one of those who would practice dwarf-tossing if given the opportunity.

No way. I rarely engage in strenuous physical activities, and tossing a dwarf strikes me as being more than I care to undertake. A baby, perhaps, but not a dwarf.

One of the phone-caller's demands was that negative use of the word short be eliminated or at least modified. He mentioned shortsighted, shortchanged, shortwinded and short-minded.

"Shortminded?" I said. "I don't think that's a legitimate term."

"Oh, yeah," he said, proudly but defensively, "just keep your ears open and you'll hear it used in a highly derogatory manner. Unless you're short of hearing."

"I think you mean hard of hearing."

"Don't mess with me."

Well, OK, maybe they are negative terms, but Short Cake didn't say what they ought to be replaced with.

In the 1960s, black activists decided the word Negro was a white word and wanted it eliminated, and away it went. They said black is black and it's beautiful and that's the way it is.

Shortly (you'll forgive the expression) thereafter, feminists demanded that sexist elements of the language be corrected, and away went chairman, councilman, manhole cover and man the lifeboats, man. In popped Person.

But if a man isn't short, what is he?

I went around asking several short people, one of whom demanded that I first define short. I said any male over the age of twenty-five who is under five feet five inches. It was an arbitrary choice.

I had no idea how tall this particular man was until the little fella glared at me and said, "I don't consider that short."

I looked down on him, so to speak, and replied, "Well, I guess it depends on point of view. Yours happens to be lower than mine."

He didn't think that was a very funny joke and called me an obscene name, so I moved on. Short people, as it turns out, have nasty little tempers. I could have said they were short-tempered, but I didn't. Well, I guess I did, but what the hell.

I hadn't realized until now that short people felt so strongly about being short. I am not tall myself, although I am over the arbitrary short-limit. What I lack in height, however, I make up for in bluster and swagger.

But even bluster and swagger do not compensate for the fact that I am less than six feet tall, a shortcoming for which my son, alas, will never forgive me. He wanted taller genes. I heard him tell his mother once that he wished she had married Larry Bird.

Back to the problem: With what word does one replace short? I asked a friend and he suggested we replace it with skimpy. Another offered economic. A third said Negro.

Negro?

"Sure," he said. "We can thus reintroduce a word that was already in existence and avoid the necessity of having to invent a new word. Negro is sort of a word-in-waiting, without current meaning."

"That won't do," I said, trembling at the very notion. "When someone asks if you're short or tall, you can't reply, 'Negro.' "

"But it won't *mean* Negro," he argued, "it will mean short."

"No sale."

Then one day I was in a movie theater, and I ordered a Diet Pepsi.

"You want regular, large or super?" the girl behind the counter asked.

"Small," I said.

"We don't have small," she said. "We have regular, large or super."

"I want the smallest one."

"We have regular, large . . ."

"I know, I know. Give me . . ."

Then it hit me. Not short, medium and tall, but regular, large and super!

"You've done personkind a great favor!" I said, leaving the theater.

From now on, there are no short men. Just regular-sized guys.

"That ought to hold the little suckers," I said to my wife.

"Maybe from now on," she said, "you'll lay off physical humor."

Fat chance.

THE SNAKE DIDN'T UNDERSTAND

It's rattlesnake season in the Santa Monica Mountains. This may not impress those who live in Beverly Hills, but if you're out hiking in the boondocks around Topanga or above the homeless compounds of nuclear-free Malibu, take heed. The snakes are out early this year and they're looking for trouble.

My assertion, I know, will be challenged by those who contend that a reptile—unlike, say, an outlaw biker or a member of the Southside Crips—lacks the capacity to look for trouble and will not go out of its way to engage in the kinds of antisocial behavior generally associated with higher forms of life.

"A rattlesnake," as one animal lover put it, "will not don a ski mask and rob a liquor store or get drunk and run you down in a crosswalk."

Maybe not, but they will bite rather indiscriminately and the bite can cause a good deal of misery for someone who, in the first place, was simply hiking along a mountain trail or pulling a few weeds.

I am moved to consider rattlers because of the appearance of two of them in my own backyard and to the anguish a friend endured when he was bitten.

The snakes in my yard were discovered by a worker who killed one and herded the other into a large jar. He took both the live snake and the dead one with him when he left, for what purpose one can only imagine.

Perhaps, as my wife suggested, he will eat one and use the other for an exciting new form of worship.

The friend who was bitten is Ollie Gunst. He was spraying poison oak recently around his Fernwood home and reached down to pull a clump of weeds and *zap!* Mr. Snake clamped on his little finger. Ollie spent four days in a hospital, most of it in intensive care.

When I asked him how it felt, he said, "Boy, that was a bummer." Ollie is Danish and the Danes are not known for either their ebullience or their poetry. That the bite, however, was an occurrence he would not care to repeat came through loud and clear.

A woman in the area who protects All Living Things suggested that the rattler was reacting naturally when Ollie mistakenly jerked it from the ground like a clump of chickweed.

"He grabbed it by the neck," she said, "and the snake bit him. You'd have done the same thing."

My wife said later that the woman was mistaken. "You'd have never bitten Ollie," she said.

"This is a big year for rattlesnakes," Fire Department Captain Sam Hernandez told me. "We've had six calls already this spring, and that's just on my shift."

Hernandez works out of L.A. County Station Number Sixtynine in Topanga, which is called upon whenever there is a problem in the community. Last year, for instance, a firefighter used a shovel to decapitate a rattler coiled under our apricot tree.

"Most of the time we try not to kill them," Hernandez said. "We try to relocate them to isolated areas."

The firefighter who did in our snake put it another way. "I'm going to have that little sucker for a hatband," he said.

A state park ranger calms rattlesnakes by talking to them. I will spare the poor woman mountains of mockery by not using her name.

"It's only my personal philosophy," she explained, as though I might misinterpret it as general state policy. No fear of that. Trans-species communication ended in California with the Jerry Brown era.

"I believe we transmit anger, love, hate and peace," she said. "If I go after a snake with intent to kill, my blood pressure goes up and my heart pounds."

"You figure a snake knows that?"

"It'll coil up and get ready to strike, won't it?" she said. "Creatures detect negative karma."

I didn't mention that last year an eight-year-old boy without a hate in his heart reached down to pet a snake and got bitten. "I wish I'd never touched it," he said later. Ollie Gunst felt the same way.

"I walk up calmly to the snake and say, 'I'm not going to hurt you,' " the ranger said. " 'I'm going to take you to a nice, safe place. I'm a ranger, so just stay calm.' "

"You tell the snake you're a ranger?"

"I try to relax him."

It was only a day later that, driving on a street near our house, I encountered another rattler.

"Stop and explain to Mr. Snake you're a newspaper columnist," my wife said.

I ran over Mr. Snake instead.

"Well," she said, looking back, "I guess he knows it now."

I guess.

PUTTIN' ON THE DOG

It seemed a shame to hear so soon after the harmonic convergence that Satan is loose in L.A., but he is.

We were only a fortnight removed from humming and holding hands and loving each other when, zap, comes news that devil worshipers are romping through the night, stealing our dogs.

If it isn't one thing, it's the other.

I learned of this from one of my regular sources, who telephoned in breathless outrage to say that the "devil people" were not only stealing dogs, but sacrificing them in their lively but disgusting rituals.

The Regular calls herself Mama Jones and loves anything with a mystical tone.

"The full moon is the worst time," she said. "You know why?"

"No," I said hesitantly, "why?"

"They go crazy with drugs and sex and want dogs more than ever."

"Well, uh, thank you very much for calling, Mama, and give my best to . . ."

"You know what they do?"

"Well, I'm sure I could probably figure it out, but . . ."

"They mix the dog blood with wine and drink it."

"Oh, for God's sake, Mama!"

"You know why?"

Before she could go further, I thanked her and hung up. Mama gets a little out of control sometimes and I was beginning to suspect this might be one of those times.

What she said, however, appears to have validity, according to both the police and the Society for Prevention of Cruelty to Animals.

An SPCA staff member said the satanic practice of stealing dogs for sacrificial purposes is, in fact, "prevalent as hell." A little secular humor there, I think.

Also, Detective Patrick Metoyer, who is an LAPD expert on satanism, witchcraft and demonology, said they often find evidence of animal sacrifices on mountain highways and near local cemeteries.

They found a dead cow once, too, Metoyer said, but he is reluctant to attribute its demise to satanism.

"Where would they keep a cow?" he asked in a puzzled tone.

By the way, the Los Angeles Police Department doesn't have a section devoted exclusively to the supernatural, although such a unit might prove handy in crimes related to the television industry, which is known to employ demonology in network programming.

Metoyer studies satanism on his own time and is often called to lecture on the subject.

He theorizes that devil worship, always a hit in England, became popular in America in the 1960s, when we were invaded by British rock stars.

"Now," Metoyer said, "we find it being practiced by kids of all ages, even down to a junior high level."

I'm not really surprised or even shocked by all this, since dancing naked around a statue of the devil is probably no worse than ripping off the people in the name of Christianity, but I am beginning to feel a little sorry for dogs.

They have always been in trouble for wandering free in parks, tipping over garbage cans, barking at night and leaving doo-doo in the street.

Then anti-dogism reached new heights of hysteria when pit bulls, for reasons of their own, began randomly chewing up neighbors and public officials, and now any dog who so much as growls at a passing cat is suspected of having homicidal tendencies.

Being pursued by dogcatchers and neighborhood vigilantes would be bad enough, but certain Asian cultures also pursue them for dining purposes. Well, no, not as guests exactly, but as entrees. And now the devil is after them, too.

I have mixed feelings.

In the first place, you are not likely to find me paying homage to any of the long list of deities and demons we traditionally honor in America, ranging from the devil to Elvis Presley.

I don't question *your* right to fall to your knees on the sidewalk before Graceland, but I'll be damned if I'll raise *my* voice in a liturgical tribute that sounds suspiciously like "Heartbreak Hotel."

Similarly, I do not worship the devil, largely because my mother hated Satan almost as much as she hated international Protestantism and spent the first ten years of my life railing against them both.

I believe, however, that those who admire the devil have a right to worship him if they choose. What they don't have a right to do, however, is chop up dogs and drink their blood with wine, even if it's a nice Cabernet served at room temperature.

A good dog is more than just a spicy beverage.

I'm not sure what we can do about it, although a friend suggests we might round up all the pit bulls in the Valley, give them to satanists to sacrifice and turn over what's left to those who enjoy dog foo yong, thereby, as he puts it, "killing two dogs with one stone."

I don't see that friend too often.

I asked a minister what he thought and he suggested everyone pray for the dogs. I guess that's better than nothing.

With God worshipers praying on one side and devil worshipers praying on the other, we will learn soon enough who is winning the battle for our immortal souls.

And all we've have to do is count dogs.

158

LIFE WITH MY 1200

My friend Billy Cobalt telephoned the other day in a panic.

"I'm desperate," he said. "My 1200 broke down. Can I come over and use yours?"

"Can't do it," I said. "It's a company car."

"Not your 6000, man! Your 1200!"

"Oh, my 1200," I said. "Sure, come on over."

It wasn't until I hung up that I realized I didn't know what my 1200 was.

I looked around the house but nothing struck me as being a 1200. I didn't even know what a 1200 *ought* to look like.

I called to my wife who was typing in the other room. "What's our 1200? Cobalt wants to use it."

"I think it's the television set," she said.

I checked. "No, that's our 2000."

"I thought the 2000 was my car."

"That's the 300," I said. "What's the typewriter number?"

"7000. We have an 8000 too."

Cobalt is in his late twenties and therefore of a generation raised under the influence of digital definition. Nothing has simply a name. We are surrounded by numbers.

I wandered from room to room. Our camera is an N2000. Our phone is a 7000. Our VCR is a 120. Our answering machine is a 1500. Our refrigerator is an 800. Our stereo is a . . . well, I don't remember what our stereo is. A 622, I think.

The doorbell rang. It was Cobalt.

"You're a real pal," he said. "I don't even *know* anyone else with a 1200."

"No problem," I replied cheerfully. "Our 1200 is always available."

"Is it working all right?"

My wife entered the room, watching with amusement.

"Just fine," I said. "It never misses a beat."

"Great," Cobalt said. "Where do you keep it?"

"I was wondering that myself," my wife said. "Where *do* you keep it?"

"I keep it," I said, stalling, "in the . . . garage!"

He looked at me with an expression of puzzlement. "You keep your word processor in the garage?"

"Oh, that," I said. "I thought you were talking about my tiller. That's a 1200 too."

"No it isn't," he replied, "it's a 3.5."

"Cobalt," I said, "just go use the damned word processor and leave me alone."

He shrugged. "Suit yourself." Then, as he headed for my workroom, he called back, "Is the 210 working?"

"Whatever the hell it is, try it."

I think I finally have outlived my potential for adapting to new eras. I did OK with the atomic era, the space age and the sexual revolution, but I am not certain I have the mental capacity for the Age of Numbers.

I have been thinking about this ever since my encounter with Billy Cobalt. Even casual descriptions are couched in numerical terms. He could have simply said my word processor or my Tandy, and I would have known instantly what he meant. My 1200 means nothing to me.

I am drowning in a digital overflow. Even the act of dialing a telephone number has assumed monstrous proportions.

I can remember a time when all one had to do was dial four numbers in order to be connected with another party.

Now, because I have MCI, I am dialing a seven-digit access number, a five-digit personal code, a three-digit area code, a three-digit prefix and only then the four-digit number I wanted in the first place. Then I ask for extension 2570.

That is a total of twenty-six numbers in order to hear my Aunt Emily's answering machine in East Oakland say she cannot come to the phone right now.

My telephone is programmable, so for a while all I had to do was push one number in order to reach Emily. But then MCI changed my code and my access sequence and I can't remember how to re-program. I am back to punching twenty-two numbers again and remembering a four-number extension each time I call.

Aunt Emily is simply not worth twenty-six numbers.

"Remember the old days," I said to my wife, "when all you had to remember was your Social Security number?"

"Sure," she said, "but you have to keep up with changing times. Retrain yourself. Think numerically."

I don't know that I am able to do that. For years I have gotten by remembering only my age, the date of my birth and my phone number. Sometimes I remember my address, sometimes I don't.

My inability to cope with the age of digits was never made clearer than when I ordered a bottle of perfume for my wife by phone.

I had to give the lady my credit card number, its expiration date, my home phone number, my work number, my address, my date of birth, the perfume's stock number and its cost. That came to sixty-one digits.

When she asked for the number of my driver's license, I surrendered.

"Lady," I said, "there is nothing in this world worth sixty-nine digits."

As I hung up, Cobalt entered from the den. "Thanks for the use of your 1200," he said. "Gimme five."

I gave him one, and it sent him flying out the door.

RECK OF THE TRIBUNE

It happened one Christmas Eve a long time ago in a place called Oakland on a newspaper called the *Tribune* with a city editor named Alfred P. Reck.

I was working swing shift on general assignment, writing the story of a boy who was dying of leukemia and whose greatest wish was for fresh peaches.

It was a story which, in the tradition of the 1950s journalism, would be milked for every sob we could squeeze from it, because everyone loved a good cry on Christmas.

We knew how to play a tearjerker in those days, and I was full of the kinds of passions that could make a sailor weep.

I remember it was about eleven o'clock at night and pouring rain outside when I began putting the piece together for the next day's editions.

Deadline was an hour away, but an hour is a lifetime when you're young and fast and never get tired.

Then the telephone rang.

It was Al Reck calling, as he always did at night, and he'd had a few under his belt.

Reck was a drinking man. With diabetes and epilepsy, hard liquor was about the last thing he ought to be messing with, but you didn't tell Al what he ought or ought not to do.

He was essentially a gentle man who rarely raised his voice, but you knew he *was* the city editor, and in those days the city editor was the law and the word in the news room.

But there was more than fear and tradition at work for Al.

We respected him immensely, not only for his abilities as a newsman, but for his humanity. Al was sensitive both to our needs and the needs of those whose names and faces appeared in the pages of the *Oakland Tribune*.

"What's up?" he asked me that Christmas Eve in a voice as soft and slurred as a summer breeze.

He already knew what was up because, during the twenty-five years on the city desk, Reck somehow *always* knew what was up, but he wanted to hear it from the man handling the story.

I told him about the kid dying of leukemia and about the peaches and about how there simply were no fresh peaches, but it still made a good piece. We had art and a hole waiting on page one.

Al listened for a moment and then said, "How long's he got?"

"Not long," I said. "His doctor says maybe a day or two."

There was a long silence and then Al said, "Get the kid his peaches."

"I've called all over," I said. "None of the produce places in the Bay Area have fresh peaches. They're just plain out of season. It's winter."

"Not everywhere. Call Australia."

"Al," I began to argue, "it's after eleven and I have no idea. . . ."

"Call Australia," he said, and hung up.

If Al said call Australia, I would call Australia.

I don't quite remember who I telephoned, newspapers maybe and agricultural associations, but I ended up finding fresh peaches and an airline that would fly them to the Bay Area before the end of Christmas Day.

There was only one problem. Customs wouldn't clear them. They were an agricultural product and would be hung up at San Francisco International at least for a day, and possibly forever.

Reck called again. He listened to the problem and told me

to telephone the secretary of agriculture and have him clear the peaches when they arrived.

"It's close to midnight," I argued. "His office is closed."

"Take this number down," Reck said. "It's his home. Tell him I told you to call."

It was axiomatic among the admirers of Al Reck that he knew everyone and everyone knew him, from cops on the street to government leaders in their Georgetown estates. No one knew how Al knew them or why, but he did.

I made the call. The secretary said he'd have the peaches cleared when they arrived and to give Al Reck his best.

"All right," Reck said on his third and final call to me, "now arrange for one of our photographers to meet the plane and take the peaches over to the boy's house."

He had been drinking steadily throughout the evening and the slurring had become almost impossible to understand.

By then it was a few minutes past midnight, and just a heartbeat and a half to the final deadline.

"Al," I said, "if I don't start writing this *now* I'll never get the story in the paper."

I won't forget this moment.

"I didn't say get the story," Reck replied. "I said get the kid his peaches."

If there is a flash point in our lives to which we can refer later, moments that shape our attitudes and affect our futures, that was mine.

Alfred Pierce Reck had defined for me the importance of what we do, lifting it beyond newsprint and deadline to a level of humanity that transcends the job. He understood not only what we did but what we were *supposed* to do.

I didn't say get the story. I said get the kid his peaches.

The boy got his peaches and the story made the home edition, and I received a lesson in journalism more important than any I've learned since.

A DAY AT THE BEACH

They're taking off their clothes in Venice again. This irritates the hell out of the cops. I heard one say, "You can't go naked in America!"

He was talking to a young woman near the old Venice Pavilion. The ocean gleamed under an afternoon sun. Diagonals of gold burnished the waves.

The policeman had just told her she had to cover her breasts. I was there watching. Not her breasts, the incident. Her breasts were, well, part of the incident.

"They take off their halters in France," the woman said. "Nobody hassles them there."

"This isn't France," the policeman replied.

"They go *completely* nude in some parts of Europe," the woman insisted.

That's when the cop zapped her with the moral imperative: "Well you can't go naked in America!"

Pow.

He was right, of course. The woman covered up and the officer, satisfied, marched on.

"Cops don't really like doing that," a man next to me said. He was there watching breasts, not the incident. "They like boobaloos too."

"I know," the woman said.

She watched the policeman until he was out of sight. Then she took off her halter again. I left right away. The right of the media to look must be tempered by domestic priorities.

What I mean is, wives seem to know instantly when their men have been in the presence of female nudity. It's an uncanny instinct God gave women in place of logic.

I walked in after that day at the beach, for example, and my wife said, "How was the skin show?" *How do they do that?*

"First Amendment rights were at stake there."

"Oh? How?"

"They were expressing themselves."

"By taking off their clothes?"

"Naked women have rights too."

"And I feel confident you will see that they are protected," she said, smiling slightly. Then she asked, "That girl in the convertible, too?"

That was different. Her naked rights almost collided with my right to stay on the road.

I was driving south on Topanga Canyon Boulevard. A convertible was coming north. A beautiful young woman suddenly stood straight up in the convertible. A passenger, not the driver.

She was naked from the waist up. She threw her arms out and as I passed, she hollered, "Hey, boy!"

I damn near drove into the creek.

Now every time someone calls his dog I turn quickly to look. *Here, boy!* A modified Pavlovian response. At least I don't drool.

I guess that's the societal problem. You let women go topless at the beach and they're going to want to go topless everywhere.

"Then," my wife said, "they're going to want to walk stark naked into the Beverly Wilshire hotel."

I tried to visualize a nude woman sashaying about in the lobby of the Beverly Wilshire.

"No," I finally said, "they wouldn't do that in Beverly Hills."

"You think they're that moral?"

"It has to do with fashion, not morality. They love clothes."

But perhaps someplace else. . . .

I let my imagination drift. I tried to think of the most fashionless place on the Westside. Not Venice. They are self-consciously downward chic in Venice. Not Malibu. They are fashion-neutral on the Golden Sands.

Culver City. Of course.

I see nude waitresses at the House of Pancakes, nude clerks at Candyland, nude dough-flippers at the Pizza Man, nude parishioners at the Foursquare Church, nude chalk-boys at the Mar Vista Bowl. They are sated with nudity, drowning in nudity, overdosing on nudity, falling, spinning into a bottomless pit of nudity. . . .

I snapped myself out of it.

"I guess you're right," I said to my wife. "You see one naked woman and you've seen them all."

"That's not exactly what I meant," she said. "And anyhow, I've been rethinking my position. I believe in equal rights. So why not . . ."

"Don't say it."

". . . nude men?"

"That's disgusting."

"Why?"

"God did not intend for men to go naked in public."

"You heard from God?"

That's what I mean about women and logic. They do not understand that men just naturally know what's right. It goes along with our ability to scratch, spit and drink beer simultaneously.

"If everyone were naked," she said, "then it wouldn't matter, would it? Only the cops would have clothes on."

"There is only one reason why everybody would take off their clothes," I said.

"To take showers?"

"To take each other. Public nudity leads to sex, not showers."

"All right, then. The police could go around and warn people not to touch in public. Nudity could be a non-contact sport."

"Handshaking too?"

"Any-shaking."

"Let's just forget the whole thing," I said. "It's getting too complicated."

167

"Does that mean you'll avoid the naked beaches from now on?"

"But the First Amend . . ."

"I'll begin a Naked Man Crusade."

"The cop was right," I said with a sigh. "You just can't go naked in America."

I'm not sure I'm ready for a nude checker at Pic 'n' Save anyhow.

A LADY IN A BOX

The woman's voice came to me from an intercom box at the foot of her driveway. "How," she demanded, "would you like someone urinating against *your* house?"

It was an intriguing question and one I might have considered at some length were I not standing in the heat of the day talking to a box.

Only moments earlier a mother and her young daughter had passed and had heard me speaking but had not seen the intercom. The mother grabbed the girl and hurried away.

I could hear the little girl asking, "Mommy, was that a pervert?" *Hush, Megan, and run!*

I was in Malibu near three state beaches that opened a year ago. El Matador, El Pescador and La Piedra. They are flanked by homes that sell for anywhere from one and a half million dollars to three million dollars. The disembodied voice lived in one of them.

She was enraged because people were wandering from the public beaches onto the private one in front of her house.

The woman had telephoned *me* in the first place. But when I went to her home, she wouldn't let me in.

"Madam," I said to her, "I am not going to stand out here on the road and talk to a box."

I felt like a customer at a fast-food restaurant.

"How the hell much beach do they need?" she demanded,

talking right over my objections. "They're like animals. Some don't even bother to crawl under blankets to have sex!"

I pictured her as painfully skinny and deeply tanned. She drank carrot juice and smoked cigarettes filter-tipped with gold paper.

It wasn't public sex or repulsive urinary habits that bothered her. She expected poor people to do that sort of thing. But they damned well better do it below the mean high tide line if they were doing it in front of *her* house.

The state has determined that beyond the mean high tide line, a private beach belongs to the public. Because the line varies, this has come to mean where the sand is wet. Those who live along the Malibu oceanfront do not make up what you might call an egalitarian community. They believe deeply that their property rights ought to extend at least out to the edge of the continental shelf.

The woman in the box was one of them.

"They live like pigs," she was saying of the public. "Filth scattered everywhere. Music turned as loud as they can play it. . . ."

"And sex outside the blankets," I added.

She didn't hear me because her control was on *talk* and she was not about to relinquish her strange and remote platform. Anonymity is the stuff of bravado.

I listened to her for a few minutes more, then left. Even as I drove away, she was still talking. The intercom box trembled with her rage.

I visited the beach nearest her home. It was difficult to find because someone had spray-painted over the state sign. I am told that once in a while a sign is torn down. The rich mean business.

They call them pocket beaches. Quiet coves at the end of pathways that wind down to the ocean from grassy slopes. Fences define the borders. Signs say, PUBLIC BEACH ENDS.

I saw no garbage. I heard no loud music. No one wandered up off the wet sand to the golden homes and urinated against the private pilings. It was too hot for sex.

What the box-woman called "the Ugly People" were exceptionally well behaved. Perhaps they sensed my presence. The poor, it is said, retain instincts that more civilized primates lose as they evolve up the economic scale.

No doubt the moment I left, debauchery ran rampant. They're cunning, all right.

"Come back on the Labor Day weekend," the woman had said. "Then you'll see."

It's an imperfect world. Passersby rest on my split rail fence and knock down the top rail. I have put it back up a hundred times.

I was beginning to get crazy about it. Every weekend it was the same thing. One Sunday I sat in the window and waited, peeking out from behind drapes.

"Why don't you buy a rifle with a scope on it?" my wife asked. "Then you could shoot them right off the top rail." She leaned close to the window, squinted, pointed a finger, and went *pow!*

I got her message. I left the window. I opened the drapes. I went about my business. That night, I checked the fence. A top rail was down.

It's the old territorial imperative. A turf mentality. Or, in Malibu, a beach mentality. The ocean is theirs, by God.

I stood on the wet sand looking up at the golden ghetto. A face appeared briefly in a window. I knew it was the woman in the box. The soaring design of her three-million dollar home created the sensation that it floated over the beach.

But it wasn't the beauty of wood and glass that impressed me. It was the ferocity of hate that radiated from the face in the window. Distance and the brevity of its appearance could not conceal the antipathy that burned across the dry sand.

I left feeling sorry not for those who are the targets of her rage, but for the remote and distant woman herself whose hate must inflame the world she inhabits.

It was, at least, clear why someone might urinate against the side of her house. They were only trying to put out the fire.

LO, THE SILENT INDIAN

Henri Towers stood in the living room of his small Hollywood apartment, resplendent in an Indian war bonnet. The trailing feathers reached all the way to the floor and then some. They were of vivid reds and yellows and oranges, and if you squinted your eyes it was easy to evoke the impression that Henri was silhouetted against a Malibu sunset filtered through smog. Once the bonnet was in place, he spread his arms and said, *"Ta-da!"*

"Hey," I said, "that's uh, really lovely." Well, it was in a way.

"Almost four hundred bucks' worth of feathers," Henri said, stroking them. "It's my favorite."

Then his face went blank, his eyes glazed over and he stood absolutely still. It was clear that I was in the presence of greatness. For this was Littlebird, the Cigar Store Indian.

Littlebird is the name he uses when he plays a human mannequin in front of Foster's Indian Store.

He is known as Ricky Randy when he is performing as a screen extra, but at the moment he was demonstrating how he is able to remain motionless.

"Just last year," Henri had explained earlier, "I stood for five hours without moving, breathing or going to the bathroom."

What he meant, of course, is that he kept his breathing shallow, which is what he was doing at that very moment. I don't know about the bathroom part.

"That's good," I said, applauding Henri's Indian freeze,

thinking that he would then thank me and we would get on with the interview.

It became clear after a moment or two, however, that he was not about to let me off the hook with just a cursory demonstration of his skill. So I looked around his apartment while he stood motionless near the television set, his close-cropped white hair gleaming in the morning sun that streamed through a window.

His apartment is in a black-and-white motif, right down to a white war bonnet flung over a naked statue of David in one corner. LITTLEBIRD is written in Indian beads on the front of the bonnet. Henri has ten bonnets and fourteen Indian outfits, including one that is made of fringed French silk, dyed Kelly green. He wears it on St. Patrick's Day.

"You must have a fortune in costumes here," I said.

Henri didn't move a muscle and he didn't say a word. It occurred to me as I stood there watching him that the man might be trying to equal the motionless record set by William Fuqua. Fuqua remained continuously motionless for eight hours and thirty-five minutes. He is to human mannequins what Babe Ruth was to baseball.

But as Henri had explained earlier, when he was still among the living, the *Guinness Book of Records* permits you to blink and swallow.

"When I remained motionless for five hours last year, one hour and five minutes of it was without blinking," he had said. "I wrote to Guinness and claimed the record for the longest period without moving while not blinking. They never answered."

I looked closely at him. He certainly wasn't blinking. I could also discern no swallowing. That is another function Henri has managed to control.

However, if he thought I was going to spread my interview over eight hours and thirty-five minutes while he didn't move, speak, breathe, blink, swallow or go to the bathroom, he was wrong. None of my functions are under very good control.

"All right," I said in a firm voice, "we probably should get on with this."

Nothing.

"For God's sake, Henri, move!"

Notwithstanding the irritation I was beginning to feel, I admire people who, as it were, go for the gold. Take Bozo Miller, for example. Bozo is a friend of mine. He is in the Guinness book for having eaten twenty-seven chickens at one sitting.

I had dinner with Bozo one night in Oakland. It was like watching the performance of a great athlete. The flow of movement from plate to mouth, the tilt of the fork, the ripple of jaw muscles. When Bozo ate, the world stood still.

However, three entrees of prime rib is all I'm going to wait for anyone. I wouldn't sit through a fourteen-inning game either. Bozo, a very tidy fat man, was dabbing at his lips with a napkin and looking for the waiter when I left.

Back to Henri. He is sixty-four and was born in Gary, Indiana, which, as he pointed out, also claims Michael Jackson, Tom Harmon and Karl Malden. He is a widower and when I asked if he lived alone, he replid, "Usually."

Henri did some photo modeling when he was young, which is where he learned to hold still. He's been holding still a good part of his life ever since. He is paid sixty-five dollars an hour for remaining motionless, with a two-hour minimum. Eight hours, five hundred dollars.

"I spook people," he said in a conversation that seemed ages ago. "I hold still, they think I'm fake and touch me." An impish smile. "I touch 'em back."

Women faint and strong men tumble backward to get out of his way. They think he's the living dead.

"Well, Henri," I said, "I want to thank you for your time and your motionlessness."

Not a flicker.

"One of these days, I'll get you together with Bozo Miller. You'd be quite an act."

After I left, I peeked in a window. Littlebird the Cigar Store Indian had still not moved. No breathing, no blinking, no swallowing, no bathroom.

It was beautiful.

LUNCH WITH JERRY

Jerry Rubin was in the forty-ninth day of his fast for peace when we met at the Rose Cafe, a gathering place for decent middle-aged ladies, unwashed intellectuals and lumbering weightlifters from a nearby gym.

His fast was to end the next day and I questioned the wisdom of an interview conducted at a lunch he couldn't eat.

"You sure you want to meet at a restaurant?" I asked as we walked in the door.

The cafe is in Venice, not far from Rubin's beachfront home.

"No problem," Rubin said. "This is my fourth fast. I can handle it."

He was gaunt and jittery and his pants were loose from not having consumed anything but water, juice and herbal tea for over four weeks.

We sat in a corner. Nearby, a heavyset man ate pasta with a languor that bordered on slow-motion.

A woman to our left made loud smacking sounds as she chewed what appeared to be a pastrami sandwich.

I felt as though we were in a Brian De Palma movie.

"Watching people eat makes me feel good," Rubin said, staring at the chicken salad I had ordered.

His eyes shone with a mad hunger. I was certain that at any moment he would smash me aside and grab my wheat roll.

"I feel guilty eating this way," I said, taking a bite.

"Hey, man, don't," Rubin said, following the path of my fork from plate to mouth. "Eating is a beautiful thing."

His mouth moved slightly as I chewed.

"Is that a carrot you're eating now?" he asked.

"Right," I said.

"That's what I thought. You can't quite tell with the dressing on it that way. It could be chicken. That must be chicken over by the tomato. Is that a slice of cucumber next to it?"

"Look, Jer, if you want . . ."

"No, no, go ahead," he said. "I insist."

I shrugged and took another bite and he said, "Man that's nice."

Rubin is forty-three and has been working on behalf of peace for a dozen years. He is not the Jerry Rubin, by the way, who was a 1960s yippie. *That* Jerry Rubin, the last I heard, was running a disco in New York.

This Jerry Rubin is still marching and singing and picketing and fasting for peace.

His latest fast had begun as his wife was preparing fried matzo for dinner during Passover. Her cooking abilities had nothing to do with Rubin's decision to go on a hunger strike. He was fasting to renounce war toys and violence-themed television cartoons.

He would declare the fast over on its fiftieth day not because peace and harmony suddenly prevailed in the world but because he had never intended to starve himself to death in the first place, and that was beginning to seem like a distinct possibility.

"Why fast at all?" I asked as we sat in the Rose Cafe on the forty-ninth day.

He continued to follow the path of my fork from plate to mouth and back again. I felt like a contestant in an eating match.

"I wanted to sacrifice something very dear in order to make a statement," he said. "Food is very dear. Also, you get media coverage when they think you might die."

"You haven't cheated at all?" I asked. "Not a bite?"

"Not a morsel," Rubin said. "I've been surviving on imaginary calories."

176

"You *pretend* you're eating?"

"Sure. Sometimes I chew popcorn in my head. I love it. We went to a movie the other night and I couldn't concentrate because of the popcorn smell."

"What are you looking forward to eating when the fast is over?"

"Pasta dripping with sauce," he said. "I dream about taking a mouthful of spaghetti and letting it sit in my mouth for five minutes before chewing it."

The sheen in his eyes intensified. If the day had gone suddenly black, they would have glowed in the dark.

This was Rubin's longest fast.

Of the others, one lasted twenty-five days, the second thirty days and the third twenty-two days. All were somehow related to peace.

"I'm beginning to forget how to chew," he said. "God, I hate water."

One of the reasons I like Jerry Rubin is that I have never met anyone quite so dedicated to peace. Others come and go, riding the crest of the movement's popularity, but Rubin just keeps at it, year after year.

He's not getting rich at it. His salary is determined by what he can raise during fund drives as director of L.A.'s Alliance for Survival. During days of flagging national interest, that amounts to very little.

"You ever think of just getting a regular job?" I asked.

"I think about it during the bad times," he said. "People say I ought to write a book or something. But I'm a high school dropout with no skills. I don't even know how to type."

I'm not sure that fasting or picketing does anything to help in the quest for world peace. But I respect a guy like Rubin for trying.

We left the Rose Cafe.

"I bet you're glad I'm done eating," I said.

"Didn't bother me a bit," Rubin replied.

We walked a little ways and then he said, "But would you mind describing exactly how chicken tastes in a salad?"

SEX ON MY MIND

When I was a kid in Oakland, everything reminded me of sex. I had some of my best erotic fantasies while eating fried potatoes or climbing trees.

I'd be halfway up the old eucalyptus out front and, whammo, a vision of Geraldine Mock would flash through my mind, naked and panting, and send me crashing to the ground.

My mother would say it was the devil's work and if I kept thinking of things like that I'd get pimples.

It wasn't until I was seventeen that a teacher informed me it was the fried potatoes, not sex, that caused pimples. What a relief.

That was a long time ago, and, while I don't eat fried foods or climb trees anymore, I am still interested in sexual fantasies, if only for statistical purposes.

Take, for instance, a survey conducted in a psychology class at Boston University. I heard about it on the car radio the other day as I was driving along the Simi Valley Freeway thinking about something other than potatoes.

The survey concluded that men have eight sexual fantasies a day, while women have only four and a half. I don't know what half a fantasy is, but one assumes it involves a person of the same sex.

I began wondering how the classroom average would compare to the city room of a daily newspaper so, through the magic of electronics, I transmitted a message asking how many sexual fantasies staff members had in an average day at the *L.A.* By God *Times.*

Twenty-one men and nineteen women responded, but I was not able to come up with an average due to the convoluted replies.

For instance, a data programmer said he had forty sexual fantasies a day but they only involved computer terminals. The sexual fantasies of a particularly egotistical reporter were all about himself.

A militant feminist responded that her whole life was a sexual fantasy because she wanted nothing to do with men, and another said she was six months pregnant and was trying not to think along those lines at the present time.

What I have decided to do, therefore, is forget about trying to reach an average and simply share with you the kinds of responses I received regarding what one respondent called spectral sex.

This in itself offers shocking insight into the truly sick and perverted people involved in producing a daily newspaper.

Sports writers, by the way, are not included in the survey since they are in a constant state of arousal and would throw any effort at honest evaluation into disarray. It has to do with the residual effects of sweat and locker rooms.

Some responses:

From a man: "My ex-wife is a Boston U. graduate. She had a dozen sexual fantasies a day and usually acted out ten or eleven of them. Occasionally, one or two would involve me."

From a woman: "I have four and a half sexual fantasies a day, and in them I fantasize about men fantasizing eight times a day about me."

Man: "I just got married and am no longer allowed to have sexual fantasies. However, I do encourage people to engage in safe fantasies by using a condom."

Woman: "Does picturing how someone would look in bed

179

with another particular person and laughing about it count as a sexual fantasy?"

(That's sexual humor, I think.)

Man: "I had one a few months ago. I think it was February or March."

Woman: "Every morning at five-thirty and every night between eight and midnight. Please don't use my name."

Man: "Who has the time for sexual fantasies? I'm lucky if I get lunch."

Woman: "I probably average three a day. Elevators and traffic on the Ventura Freeway seem to stimulate them."

Man: "They fluctuate in inverse proportion to the number of actual experiences."

Woman: "I'm dieting, and my husband says I have the 'Double-H Whammy.' I'm hungry and horny all the time."

I call special attention to the next response because of the obvious pathology involved:

"OK, details. I'm in a zoo, soaking up the sights, sounds and smells of large mammals. Suddenly a group of schoolchildren walks through. Two nuns are arguing about transubstantiation. Suddenly an elephant . . ."

Fortunately, the man is an editor and in no position to influence thought or opinion.

Woman: "I only have one a day, but it lasts twenty-four hours."

Man: "The question invades personal privacy beyond the pale and should only be asked of those seeking high political office."

Woman: "Before or after breakfast?"

Man: "Does a fantasy have to have a beginning, middle and end, or can it just be a fleeting thought? If it's a fleeting thought, should it . . . ?"

Never mind.

Several replied that it was none of my business what their fantasies were since I was not part of any of them, even those involving trees and fried potatoes.

On the whole, I suppose it wasn't a very scientific survey,

but at least it did cause a number of people to reassess their eroticisms.

At this very moment, in fact, I am looking directly at a sports writer who is staring into space and drooling slightly.

He's probably playing in a naked Super Bowl with an all-girl team. Way to go.

WHEN A TROLL DINES OUT

I have never been a person who has lived high on the hog, even during those rare good moments when the hog, as it were, was within biting distance.

I am talking about instances when I have sold a book or a script and the extra cash has allowed for a certain *douceur de vivre* beyond that which I could normally afford.

Writing for a newspaper, contrary to popular belief, is not the kind of endeavor likely to bump one onto a level of income equivalent, say, to that of a moderately successful plumber.

Bylines are fun, but they get us no closer to the hog.

Which brings me, however circuitously, to today's subject: how to tour Woodland Hills on three hundred and sixty-two dollars a day. Swagger along as best you can.

I decided it would be a grand idea to spend a night in the new Warner Center Marriott in order to evaluate the gleaming white wonder that sits like a doge's palace in the suburban splendor of the San Fernando Valley.

It may have been, however, the wrong day to involve myself in any kind of social activity, especially in an environment that required both a polished behavior and a dilettante's attitude. You can't be a dilettante when you drool.

That afternoon, I had a tooth crowned, which required shots of Novocain. Novocain, sad to say, causes me to drool while simultaneously distorting my mouth into an appearance of twisted rage.

I come across looking a little like a depraved troll.

That might explain the attitude of the hostess at Pearls, one of those overpriced, off-the-lobby restaurants that chain hotels are creating in order to outgrow their own image. The lady wouldn't talk.

While I grant you I myself might be reluctant to chat with a drooling old troll at the corner of Hollywood and Vine, I would at least exchange a word or two with a troll who walked into my restaurant willing to spend money.

The woman at Pearls, however, chose not to and led me to a table in grim silence. I didn't expect "Hail to the Chief," but a quick nod would have been nice. I felt as though I had invaded her shower.

But I do understand that those who work at gourmet houses often mistake arrogance for sophistication, silence apparently being an element of that interpretation, so I said nothing in return. I doubt that we had much to talk about anyhow.

I simply followed her, shuffling and drooling, to my table and ordered champagne, which has a way of taking the edge off most unpleasantries. I did not, however, order champagne in a chipped glass.

I am prepared to accept a good many inconveniences in life, including wooden outhouses and canned hash, but I am *not* prepared to accept *Comte d' Ussey* served in shattered crystal at a restaurant where even the asparagus is à la carte.

The waiter apologized and brought me another glass, which although it solved my immediate problem, did nothing to sweeten my rapidly souring attitude. Even a decent dinner found me churning.

But, as they say in Oakland, there is no outlook that cannot be improved with a good drink or a straight flush. I ordered a snifter of cognac, hold the chip.

The waiter explained that, although they did not have the cognac I ordered, which was Courvoisier, they did have something called Louis XIII, which he recommended as a replacement.

I said sure and sipped it without thinking much about it. And then I got the bill.

As I explained at the outset, I am not all *that* familiar with the high part of the hog. Dinner was expensive enough, but at least I had some idea of what was coming.

I was not, however, prepared to pay fifty dollars for a damned drink.

Do you realize the hell I'm going to have to endure to get a fifty dollar drink through on my expense account? An editor once told me he could eat for a week on fifty dollars, which is understandable, since he celebrated his twenty-fifth wedding anniversary at the Sizzler.

He will look at my expense account, his face will go crimson, and he will say, "Now see here, Hernandez," often confusing me in rage with one of the other Mexicans on the assembly line. I dread the encounter.

When I asked the waiter what the hell was going on, he explained that it was *very* good cognac and I explained that it was a *very* bad idea not to warn me in advance. He shrugged.

By the time I reached my one hundred and eighteen dollar room with walls so thin I could hear a door slam half a mile away, I was in the kind of mood that required outlet. I telephoned a friend, turned to reach for a pencil and yanked the plug-in phone right out of the wall.

I stood there staring. The night had assumed the tone of a Laurel and Hardy comedy. Even *I* had to smile.

What the hell. The hotel was new. Things go wrong. Settle down, Hernandez.

Good advice. I took a shower to relax. As I reached for a towel, I sneezed. The whole damned towel rack, an elaborate, multi-tiered device, slipped its fixture and went crashing to the floor.

I fixed it all right, but I think next time I will stay in Oakland.

GHOSTS IN THE SMOKE

Every time I drop by a comedy club to see what's going on I get flashes of a nightmare. I see a nice little guy on stage telling jokes in a room about half as big as a warehouse and colder than a tomb in the winter. There are only four people in the audience and none of them think the kid is funny. Even his girlfriend just stares.

I am there because the guy invited me specifically to check out his act. He is maybe twenty-six years old, small in stature and diffident in manner, the kind of person you'd expect to see working in a shoe store.

He plays directly to me, the newspaper columnist, giving it everything he's got, which is nothing at all. I try so hard to force laughter that my jaws ache. I clap so enthusiastically for no reason that my palms burn.

I am, in effect, an audience of one, because no one else in the room is even listening to the guy. Afterward, he comes up and says, "Well, what do you think?"

I stare.

It was no nightmare. This really took place during a rainy, open-mike night at a club called the L.A. Cabaret. I don't remember the kid's name, but I wouldn't use it if I did. That's the most I can do for him.

When he asked what I thought I should have used the old show biz rejoinder and said, "Don't quit your day job." Instead

I said oh, er, um, gee, uh, polish up the old act blahblah-blah. . . .

If you're looking for a punch line, forget it. The guy didn't turn out to be Steve Martin or Jay Leno. He turned out to be Mr. Nobody on a rainy night in the Valley.

I mention him because I've been checking the funny-circuit again, and he keeps haunting me, like a ghost hovering in the smoke. The most unfunny comic I've ever known, and I've known a lot of them over the years.

They're all different kinds, these people, some so manic and depressed in real life they can't tie their shoelaces without a standing ovation.

Others, like Steve Allen, are quiet and intellectual off-stage. Woody Allen mumbles and looks at his knees when he talks to you. Bob Hope seems perpetually bewildered. Shelley Berman can't say hello without making me fall down laughing.

Anyhow, I stopped by a club called At My Place in Santa Monica not long ago to hear a Jewish cowboy singer-comic named Kinky Friedman. He's kind of a manure-kicking Tom Lehrer, singing about things you hate to remember but don't dare forget.

Lehrer, for those who've never heard of him, was the best satirist who ever put words to music, but gave it up halfway through a song because nothing seemed funny anymore.

I make the comparison because one of Friedman's ballads is a piece called "Ride 'Em Jewboy." The room is bouncing along to it when suddenly everyone realizes it's about the Holocaust, and the club gets as quiet as a hayride in Hell. The impact is devastating.

Then he sings, "They Ain't Making Jews Like Jesus Anymore," and you laugh so hard you almost gag on your Scotch, until he pauses for effect, twangs a note and says softly, "We don't turn the other cheek the way we did before," and the laughter dies in your heart.

Hey, I didn't mean to go serious on you. I was just leading up to an evening spent in America's oldest comedy club, the Ice House in Pasadena.

The club was celebrating its thirtieth anniversary, which is why I was there, talking to owner Bob Fisher about humor and things.

People like Robin Williams have played there and Lily Tomlin and the Smothers Brothers and so many others I'd need two days to list them.

The reason the Ice House has lasted all these years is because there's a kind of magic to the room, a combination of warmth and proximity that turns a hard day mellow.

Also, Bob Fisher is a smart son-of-a-gun, and books all the acts himself.

Humor, he was saying the other night, is less intellectual than it used to be, but that's because the audience is too. They aren't the 1960s people digging Mort Sahl in the days before he canonized himself.

They want prop comics now and guys who hit you with ten jokes a minute.

"It's an age of MTV and sound-bite politics," Fisher said. "The comics do it less with wit today than personality and energy."

Maybe so, but a couple of guys I'd never heard of, Ron Pearson and Jack Thomas, had the room vibrating when I was there. I laughed so hard my jaws ached. I clapped so enthusiastically my palms burned.

And I kept thinking of another unknown, Mr. Nobody on a rainy night in the Valley, punching away to the hard, cold sound of one man clapping, and I kept wondering what he's doing now.

Selling shoes, I guess, and hustling dreams.

SWEET BOULEVARD BLUES

I was rolling along Ventura Boulevard the other day when a man driving a red car cut in front of me. Or perhaps I cut in front of him. It was never quite clear, I suppose, who did what to whom, but I was convinced it was his fault. I honked, cursed and shook my fist.

He, on the other hand, was convinced it was *my* fault, so naturally he honked, cursed and shook his fist.

It did not end there. Our destinations continued along the boulevard and on occasion we found ourselves side by side, he in his evil red car and I in my white purity.

At a stoplight on DeSoto, I rolled down the window and shouted: "You ought to damned well learn how to drive!"

He rolled down his window and yelled: "You can go straight to hell!"

"Say that again, mister!" I roared, sitting as high up in the seat as I could.

"Go straight to hell!" he said again, and as the light changed he zoomed off in a cloud of arrogance.

It was bad enough that the fool had twice told me where I could go, but to have said that and then beat me at the signal was almost too much.

I caught up with him and we yelled some more and gestured in a raised-finger manner which feminists in Los Angeles are known to call the Gloria Steinem Salute.

The game seemed over by then because I had to make a left

turn, but then he made the *same* left turn, honking his horn madly as he shot by me.

In about a block, however, his lane of traffic came to a stop, so I shot by him in Sweet Purity, honking and laughing with the joy of a sadist chain-whipping his sister.

This sort of highway hallelujah is a tradition among American men. It is, in fact, therapeutic for those of us in L.A. who spend so much time in our cars. Shouting, cursing and gesturing beats hell out of drowning in the vacuous babble of disc jockeys.

Usually, it goes no further than a lot of transitory male rage. I am not sure how women will work it out over the years, since they are creatures with genetically muted concepts of logic, and might end up killing one another at the curb side.

Men can handle a little hostility without coming apart, but women cannot. It has to do with the menstrual cycle.

Anyhow, the guy in the red car continued on my path for another mile or so. This surprised me, for these kinds of rolling confrontations are usually over after a block or so.

We were mutually committed by then to continue in our shows of bravado, the way a baboon jumps up and down and screams until what he perceives as a predator leaves the territory.

Fortunately, however, I saw the street I was looking for and made a right turn. I could relax a little. But then I glanced in my rear view mirror and there he was again, turning right.

At this point, on the rare occasion when it has occurred, I begin to get a little worried. I sit up even higher in the seat, clamp my teeth together and scowl, all of which are intended to convince an enemy he might be dealing with a homicidal maniac.

I noticed as I passed him, however, that he too was sitting up higher in his seat, his teeth were clamped together and he was also scowling. He was giving the homicidal-maniac stance right back to me.

"You dog brain!" I said more or less to myself, and I could see him saying "Jerk!" more or less to himself.

At last I was at the market my wife had sent me to. I gave a last angry wave and turned into the driveway and parked.

189

That's when I noticed the red car also pulling into the driveway.

Damned if he didn't park about three cars away.

I said to myself this is it, the guy really is a drooling killer looking for fresh meat. I hunched slightly and turned toward him, ready for anything.

As he emerged from his car, he saw me and hunched slightly, facing me.

We must have sensed simultaneously, however, that there was no real danger here. We were both, to begin with, not very big, so even if there had been a vicious bare-handed attack by either man, little damage would have occurred.

Our very demeanor once outside the steel and horsepower of our individual cars changed dramatically.

What had happened, I decided, was a one in a million occurrence. Two strangers whose egos had clashed in a chance encounter had, by mad caprice, ended up at precisely the same destination.

He must have realized at about the same time what had happened, unhunching even as I unhunched and trying to think of what to do next. Someone had to do something, so I said: "Nice car."

He said: "You got a good pickup there."

I said: "You've got rocket power."

He said: "I bet you get great mileage."

We nodded appreciatively and then I said: "Well, have a nice day."

He said: "Hey, yeah, you too."

And then we went into the market and he held the door for me while I entered and I let him take the first shopping cart.

We were very sweet and polite out of our cars. That's the way men are.

Thank you very much.

HILL STREET BLUES

My wife and I were walking down Hill Street near the Jewelry Mart when she stopped dead in her tracks and looked at me.

"Do you realize," she said, "how often you hum?"

"What?"

"You hum."

"I do?"

She nodded, trying to smile, though I could see it was difficult for her.

"You hum these tuneless things whenever you're walking or driving. Sometimes you even hum when you read."

"I hadn't realized it," I said. "I'm a happy person, I guess."

"No," she said thoughtfully, "you're not. You've never been a happy person. The kind of humming you do has nothing to do with happiness. It's really sort of . . . you know . . . pointless, like a dog barking at the wind."

Having gotten that off her chest, she said cheerfully, "Well, shall we go into the Jewelry Mart?"

"Wait a minute," I said, following her inside. "Like a dog barking at the wind?"

"I meant it constructively," she said, trying on a ring. "Sometimes if we realize what our annoying habits are, we can correct them." Then she added, "Before it's too late."

It hit me like a bolt of lightning. *The War of the Roses.* We had seen the movie the night before and she had been acting funny ever since.

I stood back slightly. Her next move might be to smash me in the face.

For those who have missed the film, it's about a marriage that spirals from sweetness to divorce. Everyone in L.A. is talking about it. Michael Douglas and Kathleen Turner are Oliver and Barbara Rose, the happy couple who end up destroying each other.

Their acrimony evolves in stages. Barbara, for instance, becomes slowly aware of Oliver's annoying mannerisms. One is that he bobs his head happily when he eats and chews to a silent rhythm.

Oliver, of course, is unaware of this harmless trait, but it doesn't escape his increasingly hostile wife. She sits across the table and glares at him.

Later, at a dinner party, she is offended by his laugh and that night calls him a name I have never before heard a woman call a man.

From then on, it's Katie bar the door.

Roses is a marvelous movie, but I am worried about its impact on my wife and on the relationships of other couples who comprise our small but genial social circle. It seems to say that husbands are boorish and it is therefore OK to attack them.

We were at a party the other night talking about *Roses,* for example, when midway through the conversation, our good friend Eva leaned over to our other good friend Fred, her husband, and said, "You're slurping, dear."

Fred's reaction was similar to mine when I was told I hummed. He said, "Huh?" I didn't say huh, but Fred is an actor and an actor's grip on culture and unscripted conversation is tenuous at best.

"Try not to slurp when you drink," Eva said, patting him gently on the arm. Fred shrugged and went right on drinking, and slurping.

A few minutes later, he interrupted Eva's monologue and said, "Maybe someone else would like to get a word in edgewise."

She said, "I beg your pardon?" Eva is a teacher and understands the value of manners, but is inclined toward verbosity.

192

"It's just that you tend to dominate the conversation," Fred said pleasantly. "You're a strong person, Evie."

Eva smiled, but there was murder in her eyes. "I've asked you not to call me Evie," she said.

Back to Hill Street. My wife and I were there in the first place so I could research a column on the changing face of downtown. The new high-rises, the new restaurants, the remodeled and elegant old Biltmore, the expanded and enticing Jewelry Mart.

Downtown is becoming a place to go, from the Garment District to Olvera Street. Even Pic 'n' Save is appearing more colorful than sleazy.

But after being compared to a dog barking at the wind, I was naturally more interested in vengeance than in researching a column.

I was grumbling and hurrying to catch up with my wife when it occurred to me that she never waited for me when we shopped.

"Why is it," I demanded triumphantly, "you surge ahead without regard to my whereabouts when we are in crowds?"

"I knew you'd come back with something," she said. "I could hear you grumbling. Well, not grumbling exactly, but muttering. You have this way of muttering to yourself. It's almost a growl."

"A growl?"

"It's all right, dear," she said, kissing my cheek. "I love you anyhow. Come along."

She took off through the crowds. I shrugged and followed, humming and muttering and realizing I had lost the war a long time ago, and we are very happy, thank you.

THE NEW (YUCK) GUY IN TOWN

Anyone who likes humor based on mucus, vomit, excrement, flatulence and incontinence, join me in welcoming L.A.'s newest contribution to scatological laughs, the one, the only, the disgusting Howard Stern. But hold the applause.

Stern, as many of you under fifteen already know, is the New York "shock jock" whose filth and impiety is now heard locally on station KLSX-FM. He competes each morning with Mark, Brian, Rick, Jay, Tom and other Western intellectuals, who occupy similar, but cleaner, positions elsewhere in L.A.

The man has bobbed into the city like flotsam on a tide of effluence, bringing with him the kind of . . . well . . . wit that has made him the No. 1 radio voice in such citadels of fun as Philadelphia and Washington, D.C.

Stern is accompanied by one Robin Quivers, who is to Stern what Ed McMahon is to Johnny Carson, i.e., a sidekick. The function of a sidekick is to do nothing more challenging than laugh. McMahon offers a guffaw, Quivers an inane giggle.

If she could coordinate enough to clap, she'd be Vanna White.

Among the subjects that trigger Quivers' giggle, for instance, is Stern's portrayal of a superhero he calls (you ready for this?) "Fartman."

While sparing you any effort to describe the sound effects of the segment, or precisely what the powers of Fartman can achieve, I will say it's rooted in the kind of humor that prevails during prepubescence but generally abates as one edges toward adulthood.

That they continue to find it hilarious in the East gives you a pretty good idea why everything on the other side of the Mississippi is in such serious decline.

I must say, however, that Stern's presence has precipitated a good deal of talk in L.A., much of it, of course, dirty. That is precisely the effect KLSX-FM is attempting to achieve in its quest to be No. 1 at any cost.

"There's a buzz going on," a station executive told me, "and when you feel a buzz, good things are coming. Howard will be the subject of conversation at every hot dog stand in L.A."

While I rarely frequent hot dog stands, I was a guest recently at a dinner party whose hostess has always been a paragon of purity. Her idea of obscenity was use of the word "heck" twice in the same sentence.

She had somehow become a fan of Howard Stern, however, and at this particular party was suddenly quoting comedian Sam Kinison on Stern's show as saying the press could kiss his behind.

Kinison, of course, did not say behind and neither did the hostess who, as I understand it, has since left her husband and now dances nude at Satanic strawberry festivals held annually on Stern's birthday. The Moonies were conceived with far less backing.

Support of a similar nature is heard with disturbing frequency on Stern's show as callers from L.A., where good taste has never been a serious impediment to comment, voice their happiness at having him in town.

Said one woman who described herself as a twenty-one year old from Hollywood, "You make my mornings beautiful." One can only imagine what her mornings normally consist of to find anything remotely beautiful on a Stern show.

Andy Bloom, who is operations manager at KLSX, says there were 3,000 calls the first week of Stern's appearance on the station, of which 80% were negative. Now, he informs us happily, they are down to 55% negative.

195

That's enough, God help us, to get him elected president.

I met with Bloom and his sidekick Scott Segelbaum the other day. They assured me if I would just keep listening to Stern I would ultimately perceive his honesty and significance.

What the man offers, they say, is satire so compelling that when L.A. begins to understand exactly what he is all about, we will cling to his every filthy word the way Matthew, Mark, Luke and the gang clung to every word Jesus uttered, thus making him the No. 1 commentator of all time.

Jesus, in his wisdom, didn't make jokes about oral sex, sodomy, lesbianism and bestiality, but that was only because they hadn't been invented yet. Today, of course, he would.

Bloom and Segelbaum came to L.A. from Philadelphia last February after elevating a station there to the top spot by bringing Stern into what used to be the City of Brotherly Love.

By insulting blacks, gays, women, Mexicans, Catholics, Jews, truck drivers, CPAs, blind quadriplegics and sexually abused children, Stern has managed to destroy a fraternal instinct that had existed in Philly for more than 300 years. But he's the most listened-to voice in town, and that's what counts.

"The beauty of Stern," Bloom says, "is he's so big, he gives us identity." One can therefore assume that what tumors did for the Elephant Man, Stern will do for KLSX. Everyone loves a little notice.

THE DAY THAT THE REDS CAME

It was the day the temperature reached one hundred and twelve in downtown L.A. I was wearing the lightest suit I own, which is one of those rumpled, off-white things favored by British black marketeers in Kuala Lumpur.

I was also wearing a Hawaiian shirt I bought at Penney's. It was drenched with sweat and stuck to my body like flypaper. I looked like hell.

That was particularly obvious because I was in one of the toniest clothing stores on Rodeo Drive, interviewing the mayor of Moscow near shirts that cost three hundred dollars each and a cashmere sports coat worth more than everything in my closet.

Even a leather chewing gum case sold for one hundred and forty-five dollars. I don't think I paid that much for my suit.

The place was Hermes, an establishment that is to Penney's what Paris is to Cleveland.

There were actually four Russians in the party and they were visiting at the invitation of the L.A. Fashion Institute of Design and Merchandising.

They straggled in about an hour late, looking more like survivors from the battle of Stalingrad than messengers of a New Russia. That's what heat and smog can do to a man.

The mayor of Moscow, Yuri Louzshkov, was not the most important Russian among them. Pavel Bounitch was. He is an economist, a member of the Supreme Soviet and the architect of perestroika.

This was whispered to me by several people in the entourage, both American and Russian, who hovered over me like bees at a honey farm.

Well, I was all they had.

No other media people showed up. It was just the Russians, two translators, two public relations people, some Hermes sales personnel and me, in my Kuala Lumpur suit.

I am thinking, at last, an opportunity to write an Important Column, which is what my leaders are constantly urging me to do. Never mind your dog-and-pony essays, they say. *We want substance!*

I will call it simply A Very Important Column, discuss perestroika and glasnost in concise and vivid terms and be invited to join the International Fellowship of Pundits. My dog and my pony will prance with joy.

But things went wrong.

Assistant store manager Elisabeth D'Chartoy presented each of the four Russians with a ninety-five dollar silk tie. While they were thanking her, she made the mistake of offering to let them exchange their ties for other designs and/or colors if they wished.

The mayor of Moscow, who looked a little like Charles Durning playing Nikita Khrushchev, said OK, or the Russian equivalent thereof, and chose another one, just like that. I've never seen a mayor make a decision that quickly.

It was a ridiculous black-and-white speckled number, but, hey, those are people raised on borscht and boiled potatoes. They've got a long way to go before they attain even my level of *haute couture*.

Two of the others also made up their minds quickly, but Bounitch, the architect of Russian perestroika, lingered . . . and lingered . . . and lingered.

I saw my Bird of Significance flutter out the window and die in the crushing heat.

Someone suggested I ought to start interviewing the mayor,

since time was fleeting and Bounitch was drifting somewhere between Ivy League diagonals and paisley prints.

If the theory of perestroika were neckties, he'd still be working on it. Every once in awhile he said, "Goot," meaning not bad, but then went on to something else.

Our translator was Sophia Lansky, who did a very nice job, but there was more than a language barrier here.

Louzshkov, being a mayor, was fluent in the dialect of diversion and managed to avoid adding anything noteworthy to the current dialogue between us and what used to be known as the Evil Empire.

He did say that the capitalistic elegance characterized by Hermes seemed to be unnecessary, but, since the store had customers, it was OK. I'm paraphrasing, of course.

He was basically saying if it sells, sell it.

What Russia needs, he added, was more of the kind of peasant clothes I was wearing; good, I mean goot, basic stuff. "Our market is thin," he said, "and so deep in its emptiness."

I tried to get a little into what appears to be an end to the Cold War and possibly to Godless Communism (do we still call it that?), but platitudes prevailed.

He is glad we are friends, he is having a fine time in Beverly Hills, and he is delighted that the Soviet Union is concentrating on the production of clothes instead of tanks. Food will come next.

Just about then, Bounitch chose a tie of golden zebras grazing on a pale blue Masai Mara and everyone marched out the door, taking my chance at significance with them.

So much for the Russian Bear. Wanna hear about my dog and pony?

ONE FLEW OVER THE TURKEY NEST

I suspected it might happen. By mentioning cat sacrificing at Halloween and turkey eating at Thanksgiving, I have incurred the wrath of animal activists within my readership zone.

They have gotten up off their knees, where they have been praying for wounded sperm whales and the souls of dead dogs, long enough to telephone and call me names.

One of them, who said she was a member of Compassion for Animals, asked angrily how would I like to have my head cut off and be served, roasted and stuffed, for dinner today?

I had to reply I would not like that at all.

"I knew it!" she said triumphantly, and hung up.

The column that got them riled made only passing reference to the fate of turkeys on Thanksgiving and to the ritual of sacrificing cats on Halloween.

My main concern in the essay was for the human wreckage on skid row and all those others who drift through life without hope of moral redemption.

The animal activists who called didn't even mention them. Let the fools shuffle by as best they can, I guess, but please, God, save the turkey.

I am not a cruel person. I do not advocate the random killing and eating of rhinos and bald eagles, of which there are too few in the world, and you will not find me slaughtering elephants on the Masai Mara.

But we are, after all, omnivorous creatures, and as such will eat anything that doesn't eat us first. The turkey, alas, falls into a category of delicacies consumed with impunity.

On that subject, one animal activist who telephoned called my attention to a letter that appeared in the *Times* several years ago.

The letter challenged the term "Turkey Day" and suggested that since we do not eat our mothers on Mother's Day, why do we eat turkeys on Turkey Day?

We should honor the bird, it concluded, instead of "twisting off the dead animal's neck and breaking its bones while swallowing pieces of the corpse."

Powerful stuff.

The caller was particularly concerned about the care and treatment of turkeys before their deaths. If we insist on eating them, shouldn't we at least provide adequate housing during their short and anguished lives?

Turkeys, the caller said, lived in "cramped wire cages" and had their beaks ripped off to avoid pecking each other "in the often cannibalistic panic brought on by their crowded living conditions."

I learned later he was getting his information from a press release issued by People for the Ethical Treatment of Animals, an organization whose members wear T-shirts that say, "I don't eat my friends."

Each to his own epiphany.

"Turkeys live a lousy life," the caller said, his voice rising, "and you're a part of their torture!"

Click.

After a day of harassment by angry people, I telephoned the National Turkey Federation in Virginia to ask if the cruelty charges were true.

"Nonsense," said Eddie Aldrete, director of public affairs for the federation.

"Turkeys are not raised in 'cramped wire cages' but in expensive, scientifically designed, environmentally controlled buildings as big as football fields."

He made it sound like a Club Med for turkeys.

Eddie went on to say that a turkey requires only 2.7 square

feet of living space to be happy but is given four square feet.

"That's more than the Japanese get on their little islands," I said jokingly, but Eddie is not one to joke about turkeys.

Later he would point out that his license plate reads EAT TRKY and his boss' plate reads GOBBLE.

"What about the charge that you rip off their beaks in a cruel and unusual manner?" I asked.

Eddie sighed. One could almost see him shaking his head, weary of answering the same old accusations.

"You clip your toenails, right?" Eddie asked. "Well, each turkey gets the top of his beak clipped once in its lifetime. The process is about as painful as manicuring your toenails."

That is done out of compassion, he said, so that the little darlings don't hurt each other.

Eddie added: "Turkeys are happy and well-treated. We do not thrive on tortured birds. Stressed turkeys produce tough meat."

Now you've heard both sides. If you are inclined to eat turkey today, eat it knowing its last days were spent in a kind of Grand Turkey Hyatt, with wine and laughter.

If you don't believe that, eat tofu, as Eddie said, and bean sprouts. I respect your right to dine as you like. Please respect mine.

We're having dolphin.

GETTING THERE THIS WAY

There is a man on the Westside everyone calls Shortcut Bernstein because he never takes a direct route. Tell Bernie that all you want to do is walk one block from Fourth Street to Fifth Street and he will know a shorter way to do it.

"All you have to do," he'll say, "is cut through the kitchen of Chin's Szechwan Restaurant, cross the parking lot, go down the alley and you're there. But don't let Chin know you're just cutting through his place. Pretend you've dropped by for lunch but suddenly remember something important you have to do before you can enjoy his lovely food and you'll be back later. Then split through the kitchen and you're on your way."

"What if it isn't the lunch hour," I say, "or if Chin's place is closed?"

"Then you can use the King Carpet Emporium," Bernie says, "but first you have to browse a little through their sale carpetry and ask to use their restroom and when you get down the hall . . ."

I would not write about Shortcut Bernstein today except that he is representative of a Los Angeles subculture that has figured out how to get from here to there when the freeways are in chaos and most of what we call the surface streets are gridlocked.

It was only after writing about my inability to drive from Topanga to downtown L.A. because of problems on both the

Santa Monica and Ventura freeways that I realized how many exponents of Bernie's philosophy exist.

I must have received fifty letters from people like Bernie telling me how I could have done it without the use of freeways. One of the letter writers said I sounded like a damned fool and probably ought not to be going downtown in the first place.

None of those who wrote, however, seemed to possess the shortcut expertise on a scale comparable to Bernie. He seems to know a shortcut that connects any two points in town, although I suspect much of it is instinct and not knowledge. Otherwise he would have to spend every waking hour studying maps.

Let me offer a modest example of Bernie's almost uncanny abilities.

To begin with, Bernie owns a car that is in a state of disrepair at least seventy-two percent of the time, so he telephones his friends to ask for rides. My turn came last week. Bernie was stranded at the corner of Beverly Drive and Wilshire Boulevard.

He called me downtown and asked if I would pick him up on the way home and drive him to Topanga. I said sure and met him on the corner. As we headed south on Beverly Drive, Bernie said, "I know a shortcut."

I said, "I figured you probably did."

"Which way do you usually go?"

"I go to Pico," I said, "and turn right to Overland. At Overland, I turn left and get on the Santa Monica Freeway westbound. If a motorcyclist without a helmet hasn't smashed himself against a guard rail, I will traverse the freeway to Pacific Coast Highway and turn right on Topanga Canyon Boulevard."

"That's crazy," Bernie said. "Pico is a mess and Overland is worst. Keep going straight on Beverly."

I followed his advice out of curiosity and began an odyssey on the most circuitous route I have ever taken to achieve a destination. It wound and twisted through Beverly Hills and Rancho Park on streets named Beverwill and Castle Heights and McConnell and Club and Motor and Wala Vista and other streets I cannot remember.

"Swear you'll never reveal the exact shortcut," Bernie said. "It'll ruin it for the rest of us."

"I swear."

Eventually we ended up westbound on the Santa Monica Freeway but Bernie said it would be crazy to go all the way through McClarren Tunnel to Pacific Coast Highway. "That's for real jerkholes," was the way Bernie put it.

He had me get off at Lincoln, cut over to Seventh and follow it past San Vicente to a street called Entrada, where we twisted down to West Channel and then PCH, which was also crowded.

"Now what," I asked, "into the ocean?"

For a moment I thought he was going to say yes.

"What you can do to avoid this mess," he said after a long moment of silence, "is to take a long cut."

"A *long* cut?"

"There's less stress to simply driving than to waiting in traffic. You go up Chautauqua to Sunset and then down Sunset to . . ."

I am not in the market for long cuts so I just stayed on PCH and eventually we got home, although Bernie sulked the rest of the way. He was angry because I ignored his advice. I would have told him to go straight to hell but Bernie never goes straight to anything. There's a shortcut to that too.

LITTLE GROUPS OF WINOS

The Bistro Garden, for those who lack entree to the good life, is a Beverly Hills restaurant where, with the proper combination of comestibles and combustibles, it is possible to spend one hundred dollars for lunch.

It is a restaurant favored by presidents of the United States, visiting dignitaries from abroad and celebrities of such stature they are able to afford cars worth more than your house.

In other words, it is not the kind of establishment where one might comfortably order a burger and a beer and expect thereafter to sit around and watch two hockey teams bloody each other on a television set over the bar.

Due to its haute cuisine, its prices and its general ambiance, the Bistro Garden quite obviously is additionally not the type of restaurant that encourages drunkenness, rowdiness or other displays of untoward public behavior.

In the twenty-five years it has been in business, there have been no complaints relative to vulgar displays of any kind, including but not limited to customers urinating against its outside wall.

Which brings me to the San Fernando Valley and to what has become known as the Battle of the Bistro.

It all began when a kind of mid-level restaurant and bar called Tail of the Cock was torn down to make way for a tony shopping center on Ventura Boulevard in Studio City. Centerpiece of the project was to be a Bistro Garden fashioned after its Beverly Hills prototype.

Ventura Boulevard, as you might know, is a humdrum collection of pizza parlors, food markets, dry cleaning establishments and other businesses of a less-than-inspiring nature.

It is not, as a friend pointed out, a Champs Elysees, a Paseo de la Reforma or even a Pico Boulevard.

Builder Herb Piken, therefore, assumed he would be greeted with kisses and angel hugs when he announced the construction of his upscale fifteen million dollar shopping center and attendant Bistro Garden.

Au Contraire.

What he got was a chorus of objections from posturing neighborhood activists who protested that his proposal would be a blight upon their block, which is difficult to perceive, the block being what it is.

The shopping center, they said, would destroy the "village" nature of Studio City and the Bistro Garden would attract drunks, bums and other defilers of public decency.

Visions of loutish millionaires in cashmere suits vomiting on the neatly tended lawns that abut the planned Bistro filled the air. Thoughts of wealthy rock stars prowling the suburbs in search of aberrant sexual satisfaction chilled the blood.

One woman told of already existing effronteries to good taste in the area of restaurants across the street from the proposed Bistro.

In one week, she said, she picked up forty wine, beer and vodka bottles tossed there by those who had not been able to sate their alcoholic thirst in the restaurants and had finished off the booze in their cars.

Further, she said, she saw a man walk across the street from the restaurants and urinate in front of her home, and anticipates that others will line up on the lawn for the same purpose if a Bistro Garden opens in the Valley.

This kind of silliness has managed to prevent final approval of the restaurant despite contradicting arguments that the Bistro does not count among its clientele those inclined to leap from their limos and relieve themselves on residential lawns.

Kurt Niklas, who owns the Bistro, calls the whole business childish and says he intends to continue the fight to open the new restaurant. Those who protest, he adds, are of an income and mentality that would not patronize it anyhow.

Neighborhood activist Eileen Kenyon huffs back that she's been to the Bistro and likes it, but "the idea that high-class people don't drink is baloney. *Everybody* drinks."

Even in the closing days of the Tail of the Cock, she said, little groups of winos were hanging out in her neighborhood, and if the Bistro opens in the Valley, she says ominously, the winos will be back.

The Bistro Garden is not a place I visit with any frequency due to the limiting nature of expense accounts offered to those of us in the trenches at the *L.A. Times*.

But since Denny's has managed to proliferate throughout the Valley with impunity, I see no reason why a restaurant that offers something considerably more appetizing than a Grand Slam breakfast ought not to receive equal consideration.

If Studio City loses the Bistro Garden, it will be left with what it deserves: a man who urinates on lawns and a little group of winos looking for a better place to drink.

KISS THE CILANTRO FOR ME

There are thousands of restaurants in L.A., including a few five stars and an abundance of others whose collations require ketchup poured over them before the food is considered edible. Even the custard pudding needs help.

I eat mostly at little Italian places on the corner, where a nameless red house wine is served in chipped glasses and one suspects the pasta may have been an uneaten portion off someone else's plate.

I got used to chowing down like that in Oakland, where a food establishment is considered gourmet if nothing on the plate moves. Members of the Oakland A's still dine at such eateries, which results in a pathological condition that obviously impedes athletic performance.

I mention this to stress that my background does not include the kind of training that would prepare me to write about food. I either like what I eat or I don't, whether it is *foie de veau* prepared by Wolfgang Puck or chili over eggs by Mama Consuela.

Which is why I was somewhat surprised to receive a letter from Carlos Haro, owner of a restaurant called Casablanca, that began, "Dear Mr. Martinez. As a food and dining expert, you . . ."

It was an invitation to judge a new gourmet dish Carlos had created. Since I had never been asked to discuss anything I ate, I said to my wife, Cinelli, "I smell a column." She said, "Poor Carlos."

It was a new experience. We found ourselves among people who could actually tell the difference between a clam and an oyster. There were restaurant critics not only from L.A., but from Mexico and Japan.

They nibbled at their food and then smacked their lips ever so slightly, as though throwing baby kisses to the air. Then they'd look off to the middle distance, savoring the subtle tones of tangy sauces.

"Isn't that beautiful?" I said to Cinelli, watching them baby kiss, then either nod in approval or make those squinty little faces food experts make when they aren't sure. "They're such cute little buggers."

"You've learned something new," Cinelli said. "Now you can baby kiss after your Big Macs."

Carlos' new creation was something called an enchiLaCa. It's meant as kind of a hip Mexican joke, see, like the "La" stands for L.A. and the "Ca" means California. Hence, enchiLaCa.

It's called that, Carlos explained, because L.A. people like to try new things, and also some enchiLaCas are filled with vegetables, which L.A. people like very much.

At least that's what I think he said. Carlos has been up from Mexico only a few years, and doesn't speak good English.

And since I don't speak Spanish at all, there was something of a communication problem.

For instance, it took five minutes for us to work out that "angreliants" meant ingredients, as in they are composed of very selected angreliants.

It took even longer to learn one of the enchiLaCas was filled with chayote. It is a tropical vine off of which grows a grotesque squash-like thing.

"Is good," Carlos explained, "but skin is look ugly."

"If you didn't drink martinis," Cinelli whispered, "you'd know what he's saying. Look at the food experts, they're only sipping a little champagne. It keeps their taste buds happy, but sober."

210

Casablanca's decor is fashioned after Rick's Place in The Famous Movie of the same name, although its specialty is Mexican food with angreliants. A star of the evening was seventy-five-year-old Dan Seymour, one of the last of the actors who was in *Casablanca*.

Dan is a big-bellied man who played the Arab guard at Rick's. He tells terrific stories about Bogart and the others, some of which last longer than the movie itself.

One of the stories was about Ingrid Bergman riding a camel, or maybe it was a giraffe. Dan began telling the story during the soup and was still telling it when the food critics were baby kissing the dessert.

We were at the same table with David Westheimer, an owlish little Texan who wrote *Von Ryan's Express* and *My Sweet Charlie,* among other best-sellers.

I guess he's something of a gourmet, which is why he was invited. He said the food was terrific, they didn't have things like that in Houston.

You can bet your royalties on that. I've been to Houston and know for a fact that many of their chefs were trained in Oakland.

The food experts give the enchiLaCas high marks. You could hear their taste buds singing *vivacissimo* in three languages as they left.

I said to Cinelli as she drove us home, "I really liked that stuff."

"Good," she said, "that will no doubt appear in subsequent ads. 'I really liked that stuff'—Al Martinez, Gourmet-in-Training.' It's a shame you don't baby kiss."

I'm working on it.

211

HONK, HONK, HONK!

When the first true automobile was tested in Paris in 1769, there was no need for a horn.

There were no other cars on the road, the steam-powered vehicle moved at the speed of a French stroll, and anyone in its way simply stepped aside.

Only when the second automobile was manufactured did the need for a horn arise.

As I understand it, the second car cut the first car off and continued on its way, causing great emotional stress to the driver of Car Number One, who was unable to communicate his rage.

He cursed, of course, but cursing in French lacks the impact of cursing in, say, Italian or Japanese, and the driver was left trembling in despair.

The car horn was subsequently developed and exists today as an essential element of highway communication and driver therapy.

"If you can't honk," a psychologist friend said to me, "frustration builds to undirected hostility, which can emerge in situations unrelated to the causative factor."

In other words, a person who can't honk could end up building his own nuclear bomb and wiping out a neighborhood.

So listen carefully. I can't honk.

There are roughly twenty-two thousand miles of public roads

in Los Angeles County which are traversed by more than six million registered vehicles, often at the same time in the same lane.

Nowhere in the world is the automobile more imporant than in L.A., due to our historic inability to put together any kind of adequate public transportation.

But without a horn, a car is nothing.

I discovered this the day I lost my honk. It happened on the Santa Monica Freeway at rush hour. My wife, the patient Cinelli, was with me.

To begin with, I am an aggressive driver who believes the lane I occupy ought to be clear for at least a mile ahead. Any car that enters it within that distance is an unacceptable intrusion and earns a blast from my horn.

This is accompanied by a brief oral description of the driver's similarity to a portion of the human anatomy that goes over the fence last, as stepdaddy used to say.

Predictably, on this day someone did cut in front of me. I cursed lustily and hit the horn. But while the curse rang out, the horn didn't.

"My horn's dead," I said, pounding on the honk pad. I couldn't believe it. No car I ever owned had gone suddenly hornless.

"I guess you'll just have to learn to curse louder," Cinelli said. "Either that, or stick your head out the window and holler, 'Honk, honk, honk!'"

I stopped at a gas station. A guy who looked like a mechanic was standing around smoking a cigar and picking his teeth at the same time. It required all the coordination he could muster.

"I think my horn fuse is out," I said.

"No horn fuse," the mechanic said.

He was a man of few words. Eighty-eight Pontiacs don't have no horn fuses. Also, it wasn't no bad connection. He checked that too.

"Then what could it be?"

"Maybe the old relay," he said.

"Where's the old relay?"

"Don't know."

"You're a mechanic and you don't know where the old relay is?"

"Ain't the mechanic," he said, "waitin' for the old missus." At which point the old missus emerged from the ladies room and they left.

"Might check the owner's manual to find the old relay," Cinelli said. "It's probably under 'O.' "

I couldn't find it, so to hell with it. We took to the road again, honkless. I felt like a man without his manhood.

Pacific Coast Highway was a mess. I cursed, yelled "honk" and shook my fist, but it wasn't the same.

At one point, road work forced us to wait twenty minutes. When it was our turn to move, the guy in front of me didn't. He'd fallen asleep.

"Maybe he's dead," Cinelli said. "Show compassion."

"I'm not smashing him off the road. That's compassion. *Honk, honk, honk, damn you!*"

I unsnapped my seat belt and was about to get out and kill him when Cinelli said, "You start a fight and you can kiss sex good-bye."

She has an interesting way of putting things.

He finally moved and I got home, but my horn still doesn't work. It's either take the time to get it fixed or build a bomb, kiss sex good-bye and wipe out the neighborhood.

I'm thinking, I'm thinking.

HULK HOGAN HEAVEN

I am sitting here on a rainy evening trying to find words that will adequately describe an activity whose prime function is to set two hulking male humans against one another in a grunting display of sweat and saliva.

It isn't sport or even quasi-sport, else it would be listed in our daily roundup of obscure physical pastimes, along with lacrosse, fencing and mackerel fishing off Marina del Rey.

It isn't exactly show biz, either, because otherwise it would be included in our carpet coverage of those activities that occur within the same week as the Academy Awards.

I suppose one could place it somewhere between sex and police brutality, in that it involves a good deal of slapping at each other in primitive foreplay followed by groaning, grappling, smashing and, ultimately, the sweaty climax of mock triumph.

I am speaking, as you may have already guessed, of something called Wrestlemania, the seventh annual convocation of which occurred Sunday afternoon in the L.A. Sports Arena.

Therein were massed sixteen thousand members of a subculture whose growing numbers may spawn a new species of *Homo erectus* with a brain equally divided between an insatiable desire for beer and a primeval need for body slams.

They yell for no reason, are often given to actually *barking* their satisfaction, and worship the ground trod upon by men of great bulk and low foreheads whose biceps measurements are often higher than their IQs.

But, still, they are a class to be studied, and into this living laboratory of barking and Budweiser strolled a quiet and a cultured man with a willingness to go where others fear to tread.

Why is it always up to me?

There were fourteen matches, as I counted them, involving costumed contenders known as Animal, Smash, Crush, Barbarian, Hitman, Anvil, Hammer and other appellations intended to denote strength and random violence.

I was there when the first bout began at exactly four o'clock or, as a fan might put it, when the big hand was on the twelve and the little hand on the four.

(You've got to bear in mind this is a wrestling show, not commencement day at the USC School of Biophysics.)

The matches themselves were of only passing interest, other than to serve as catalysts for maniacal crowd, I mean herd, reaction.

All involved bearhugs and power slams, interspersed with a certain amount of eye gouging and crotch kicking, and all had their heroes and their villains.

Because the bouts are choreographed, one of the brutes could probably perform alone as a kind of solo wrestling act, throwing himself to the canvas in feigned agony and thereby eliminating the need for even a hint of harm to anyone else.

Many are, in their way, alone in the ring anyhow.

But then, I hear you cry, what fun would it be without the tantalizing possibility of someone actually being crushed by Crush or smashed by Smash?

Well, perhaps you're right. It's unlikely that a man alone in a ring could, say, break his own arm or dislocate his own shoulder, so the matches ought to remain a duet. Tradition counts for something.

But the fans are far more interesting than the performers.

Homo wrestlemanic, as the species might be known, is raucous but otherwise harmless. Between encounters, one or two might be found grazing peacefully somewhere on a hillside.

There is even a degree of almost human sensitivity among the females.

I'm not speaking here of the woman who shouted "I want to have your baby!" at the British Bulldog, but of the lady crying softly to herself in an upper row seat.

She was perhaps eight months pregnant, and I was concerned she was, as a friend used to say, about to drop her foal. She indicated by shaking her head, however, that wasn't the case.

Through sobs she managed to communicate that her pain, her deep anguish, lay not in prenatal trauma but in the fact that Undertaker had just bested her hero, Superfly Jimmy Snuka.

Crying over a vanquished wrestler may be the ultimate form of empathy.

It struck me as I wandered through the crowd of noisy primates that everyone seemed bigger, and possibly happier, than me.

I guess that goes along with a primitive diet of roots, bark and freshly killed water buffalo, without chemicals or preservatives of any kind.

Also, as security guard Ray Heimstadt pointed out, "They have a hell of a good time here."

Ray is six foot five and weighs two hundred and thirty pounds and I wasn't going to argue with him in Hulk Hogan Heaven. Anyhow, who's to say that having a hell of a good time isn't the name of every game?

Even I feel better knowing Haku and the Barbarian got exactly what was coming to them.

REQUIEM FOR A CLOWN

For a man who had spent his life making others laugh, Martin Ragaway's final observation seemed a bitter punch line to thirty-five years of comedy writing.

Kept alive by tubes at St. Vincent's Hospital, unable to speak, he gestured for a pencil and a pad and wrote laboriously, "Game's over, we all lose."

Then, his body eaten with cancer, Ragaway closed his eyes and was dead at sixty-six. Or sixty-two. I never did know his real age.

"How old *are* you?" I asked impatiently when I first met him a few years back in a bar called Residuals.

Ragaway had been sidestepping the question for an hour, telling jokes, making comments, waiting for laughs. He had the quick, furtive moves of a chipmunk, and even sitting still seemed in motion.

"S—Sixty," he finally replied with a slight stammer.

"You don't look it," I said in false praise.

"O—k—kay," he shot back, "Fifty-nine."

Before I could respond he was out of the starting blocks again and halfway around the track with, "You hear about the widow in Miami Beach? She meets a guy and says, 'I've never seen you around here before.'

"He says, 'I've been in prison for thirty-four years. I poisoned my wife, cut her into small p—pieces and put her in the garbage disposal.'

" 'Oh,' she says, 'then you're a s—single man!' "

Ragaway never stopped entertaining. He told stories, he repeated anecdotes, he made up gag lines. Sometimes he stammered, sometimes he didn't. The faster he talked, the less he stammered.

He had his own newsletter, "Funny, Funny World," composed of jokes, offbeat news items and comments on the news. He began by sending it to friends. In a few years it had a circulation of ten thousand.

It was another way of telling a story, of defining with wry insight the nature of the existence he would ultimately call a game. Ragaway was a man obsessed with laughter, the ultimate entertainer, the quintessential clown.

Then why didn't he leave us laughing?

I last saw him three months ago. I didn't know he was dying. None of his friends did. He didn't look well, but he never looked well. That's what made my false compliment seem funny to him back at Residuals.

The face was pale and craggy, the eyebrows arched in a sad and quizzical expression, his hair dyed a funny auburn. Only the eyes were bright and riveting. Only the eyes were alive.

He talked about his years of comedy writing the last time we met, about how he churned out gags for Skelton, Benny, Hope, Gleason and a lot of others you wouldn't remember if I told you.

There was a biographical quality to his monologue. He wanted me to remember. The cancer he had secretly fought for almost two years was winning.

Ragaway had written for radio first and then television. He produced scripts for four hundred sitcom episodes, or maybe eight hundred. He told different stories. "All those episodes," he'd say with incredulity, "and I'm s—still able to dress myself and t—tie my own shoes."

He loved making people laugh but hated laugh tracks, and it drove him crazy when sitcom actors couldn't deliver the lines he sweated to create.

Of one particular performer he'd say, "She's so dumb she thinks a d—double entendre is a strong drink."

"My father was always entertaining," his daughter Jill said. "At a dinner party he'd sneak a look at a matchbook cover he'd written words on during the day to remind him of jokes. When we'd see the matchbook cover come out we'd say, 'Oh, oh, here it comes.' Then he'd start in."

Ragaway's last note perplexes fellow comedy writer Bill Larkin. "It didn't seem like Marty. He was always up. His only goal in life was to entertain. But maybe being up and entertaining just covered his *real* attitude. Who knows?"

Humor is born in dark places of the soul, masking the anguish with a tilt toward absurdity. The humorist defines not only human folly but his own dreadful inadequacies, and to come face to face with them is to look the devil in the eye.

I think at the end Ragaway was observing life's ironies more than its futilities. He was acknowledging that we all play a game we can never win, no matter how well we play it.

"Humor," he once said to me, "is based on little realities. Everything's a joke."

Last week he must have realized the joke is ultimately on the clown.

FUN WITH BUBBA, NOT JANE

To hear Bubba Smith tell it, a beautiful woman was snuggled so close to him she looked like Siamese twins. Her head was on his bare chest, the perfume in her hair adding fire to a moment dreams are made of. The night was exquisite, the mood divine.

Then she touched his chest with fingertips as light as a summer breeze and said, "Ummm, soft."

For most of us in a similar situation, it wouldn't have mattered what she said. She could have whispered, "Ummm, energy equals mass times the speed of light squared," and what the French call *l'humeur d'amour* would have remained intact. As long as the lady was willing to stay where she was, the devil take her observations.

Not Bubba Smith. Here is a man who used to toss quarterbacks around as though they were macadamia nuts. Six feet eight, two hundred and eighty-five pounds of muscle and iron coming at them down the track, throttle wide open.

Fans used to scream "Kill Bubba, kill!" as he sliced past the center like an armor-piercing shell with football teams in Michigan, Baltimore and Oakland. Some say they could hear a scream in the microseconds before impact.

And now a woman was tapping his chest and whispering "Ummm, soft."

"I didn't say anything at the time," Bubba recalled with a

frown as we sat in the lobby of an exercise studio, "but, man, that blew me away. I mean, I ain't *never* been soft."

To make matters worse, it was the lady's habit to walk five miles every morning in long, energetic strides. On this particular morning after, Bubba joined her. Later, she went off to work. Bubba sat down to rest for a few moments and woke up seven hours later.

"I suddenly realized," he says, "I was out of shape."

That was several years after his retirement from professional football. Bubba had become a successful actor tooling around town in a silver Rolls-Royce Corniche. Meanwhile, his weight had crept upward from two hundred and eighty-five pounds of muscle to three hundred and five pounds of what he calls fat and what you and I would regard as enough muscle to satisfy thirty percent of America's women.

He went on a diet of tuna and hard-boiled eggs and became a familiar figure around the gym. Very soon, he was two hundred and forty-seven pounds of muscle and iron again. At forty, he looks like an I-beam with broad shoulders. Now he wants to help all the rest of us.

I met with Bubba so that he might lobby me on his new exercise videotape, "Bubba Until It Hurts." He compares it to the Jane Fonda tape of a similar nature by pointing out that on his tape, the five women and four men sweat. Jane Fonda, it appears to Bubba, never sweats.

Accompanying him was his press agent, Bob Abrams, who is five feet eleven and weighs three hundred and two pounds, most of it situated in the immediate area of his belt. They were a strange pair. If it were a costume party, Bubba would come as a basketball player and Abrams as the ball.

"Where I come from," Bubba was saying, "women sweat." There is a certain sexuality about sweating women. Maybe they don't sweat in Hollywood, but they sweat in Beaumont, Texas.

His tape is oriented toward weathered grownups, not nineteen-year-olds with perfect bodies. All of the women on his tape are over thirty. One of the men is forty-eight. They puff when they're tired. They groan when it hurts.

I asked Abrams if he had ever exercised along with Bubba

222

and the Gang. He looked at me as though I were mad. I asked him if he exercised at all. "Sure," he said. "I get up in the morning."

Bubba observed him skeptically. "You sure?" he asked.

I am less than a perfect physical specimen. I am small and afraid. Pain shoots through my back when I lift anything heavier than a dry martini. I had to give up olives years ago because of the strain.

You could tap almost anywhere on my body and murmur "Ummm, soft," though possibly without the murmur and certainly without the *ummm*. So I bounced along with Bubba for about thirty minutes in the privacy of my own house to see if it made a difference.

I strained, I reached, I dropped into positions no decent man ought to attempt. I heard Bubba say to me from my television screen, "In order to get through it, you gotta get to it!"

It occurred to me as I lay on my back with my feet in the air and a cigar in my mouth watching Bubba between my knees that I had no further desire to get to it. Bubba and Bill and Gloria and Kim and Al and Lisa and Renee and Vince and Gail would have to get to it without me.

I lay on the living room floor, afraid that if I moved something would break. Neighbors, concerned about my absence, would call the police. Paramedics would find me rotting in front of the television set. After an hour, I struggled to my feet. Nothing would break. I couldn't move fast enough for breakage.

That evening, my loved one lay her head on my chest. Her perfumed hair set the night on fire. Music played. Her breath was hot against my body. She tapped my chest gently. "You asleep already?" she asked.

"Blame it on Bubba," I said, rolling over.

I snored. She did a crossword puzzle. The end.

KING OF THE KAZOOS

Albert Broder was in a high state of annoyance. The customer who had just walked into his office had committed the unpardonable sin of putting the wrong end of a kazoo in her mouth.

"My God," Broder was saying, "haven't you ever played a kazoo before?"

He is a large, balding man with an aggressive manner and a voice as flat and dry as a Texas desert.

His customer, on the other hand, was a small, whispery woman in her mid-thirties who was obviously not accustomed to verbal assaults by kazoo salesmen.

"Only as a child," she replied in a teeny-tiny voice.

"Where you from?" Broder demanded.

"West Covina."

"What do you do?"

"What?"

"What kind of work?"

She said she was an actress and a part-time chandelier salesman.

Broder shook his head, the implication being that he has had trouble before with West Covina actresses who sold chandeliers.

"You do it this way." He put a white kazoo with a Coca-Cola logo in his mouth. Then he played something that sounded like "Stars and Stripes Forever."

"Try it," Broder said to the poor woman.

That was when she made her second mistake, or perhaps her third, if you count walking into the store in the first place as a mistake. She *blew* into the kazoo.

"You don't blow into the kazoo, for God's sake!" Broder said, grimacing. "You *hum!*"

He demonstrated a second time, gave the woman a bag full of free kazoos and sent her on her way. She hurried out, never knowing that Broder in reality is a kind and generous man. He is just very passionate about kazoos.

"Educating the public is my Number One job," he explained with a sigh. "I even had an instruction booklet made up."

He handed me a booklet: "The Kazoo. A Fun Music-Maker for All Ages. Operating instructions: (1) Place larger end in mouth. (2) Keep fingers and thumb clear of turret and small opening. (3) Hum (don't blow). Note: If instrument fails to activate, loudly say the word *doo* into the larger end."

The instructions are accompanied by the silhouette of a man playing the kazoo properly. One can almost sense the presence of Broder just outside of the picture, watching.

Broder has been selling the instruments for three years. Before that, he drove a taxi in Detroit. He considers himself Mr. Kazoo.

You can't miss his small, kazoo-cluttered office. In front, there is an animated gorilla with a clown on its shoulders and a kazoo in its mouth. The gorilla's head moves from side to side.

I visit Mr. Kazoo occasionally to see what he's up to. He is not the only promoter I have ever known, but he is the only promoter I have ever known who is trying to be to the kazoo what Colonel Sanders was to fried chicken.

His latest kazoo-oriented undertaking involves wrestling.

"I'm looking for a wrestler I will call Captain Kazoo," Broder said. "He'll wear a Captain Kazoo outfit and hand out five thousand kazoos with his picture on it every time he wrestles. You like wrestling, I'll get you tickets."

I said I didn't want any wrestling tickets.

"I'll get you tickets to *Cats* then. You know the guy who wrote 'Mairzy Doats'? Al Trace. He's doing a special song for

225

Captain Kazoo. All I need is the right wrestler. When do you wanna go?"

"I don't want tickets to *Cats*," I said.

Broder played "Mairzy Doats" on the kazoo. It also sounded like "Stars and Stripes Forever."

"You ever hear of the Kaminsky International Kazoo Quartet?" he demanded.

I said I had not.

"They're famous, for God's sake!"

"I still haven't heard of them."

Broder scowled. "The Kaminsky International Kazoo Quartet plays all over the country," he said. "They're coming here to some colleges. They'll be using my kazoos. I'm trying to set them up to play half-time at a Lakers playoff game. You like basketball? I'll get you some playoff tickets."

"I don't want playoff tickets."

"They used my kazoos once, but they always wait until the last minute. I can't wait that long. Take a look at this."

Broder handed me a piece of flared plastic, allowed me to examine it, then took it back. He affixed it to the outer end of a kazoo so that it looked a little like a miniature plastic trumpet.

"I invented that," he said. "It's so you can tell one end of the kazoo from the other. It'll be ready in thirty days. Write that down."

"Hey, you can't . . ."

"Write it down, for God's sake."

What the hell. I wrote it down.

"It makes a different sound," Broder said. He played a tune. "You know what that was?"

" 'Stars and Stripes Forever'?"

He didn't say whether I was right or wrong. He just said, "What kind of cigars you smoke?"

"Broder," I said very slowly, "I don't want to see *Cats*, I don't want to be at a Lakers playoff game, I can't stand wrestling, I've quit cigars and to hell with the kazoo."

"Hey," he called as I stomped out past the animated gorilla, "will I see you again?"

Of course.

226

ONE EATS ITS MATE, ONE DOESN'T

An aunt from Illinois who has learned all she knows about Los Angeles by reading Mike Royko is visiting for a few days and it's driving me crazy. Forget that she is as ignorant about L.A. as Royko is. I can handle that. But she is also terribly nervous, hums all day and is visiting during the height of rattlesnake-black widow-fire season..

I picked Emily up at the airport last Monday. Her husband Wil died just a few months ago, so after we had exchanged hugs I told her how sorry I was that Wil was no longer with us.

"That's all right," she said, looking around. "He'd have hated California." I should have known it would be that kind of visit.

As we carried her luggage to the car, she stopped suddenly, pointed toward a man emerging from the terminal and asked loudly, "Is that a homosexual?"

"God, Emily," I said, trying to quiet her, "I don't know." The man had apparently heard and was glaring at us.

"Wil used to say you could tell by their small hands," she said as I hustled her away. "I always wanted to see one. Where do they keep them usually?"

"West Hollywood," I said. "Now let's go."

On the way to my house in a canyon, we passed a flatbed truck carrying a giant red bulldozer. Aunt Emily wanted to know what that was all about.

I explained it was the start of the fire season in Southern California and the fire department was getting its equipment in place. She began humming.

It wasn't until later I learned that humming is her safety valve. If she didn't hum, she would scream and cry in fear. It is an aimless little hum, without tone or destination. I hate humming.

We arrived home after dark on a star-filled evening. In the distance, a coyote howled. I could feel Aunt Emily tense up. She hummed faster.

Though she said nothing, I knew what was going through her head. We had passed a hippie on the way up. An untrimmed beard and no haircut since the 1960s covered his face with hair. She was thinking *werewolves!*

I was sorry I had told her about the doctor they arrested one night on the beach at Malibu, howling at the moon.

She looked around the house, checking each room and their closets carefully. You never knew when a homosexual or a werewolf might jump out. When she had finished, she said, "So this is where you get laid back."

"Actually," I explained, "you don't *get* laid back. One is laid back when one is, well, mellow. And I'm never mellow."

"Oh," she said slyly, "then what's *this?*" She was holding a bowl that contained a white substance. She was thinking cocaine.

"That's just powdered sugar, Em."

"*Sure* it is.

She wanted to know where the sex parties were held.

"In the back yard," I said with a sigh. There was no point in arguing. That night she hummed in her sleep.

The next day was a disaster. Normally the few dangerous creatures that inhabit the Santa Monica Mountains do not all appear at once. But they must have heard that Aunt Emily was in town.

First there was the black widow. I found it as I was showing her around the deck and killed it with a stick. No big deal. Emily was terrified. She was positive thereafter that every

228

harmless little spider we saw was a black widow, even though I had told her about the red hour glass on its belly.

"But how do you know for *sure?*" she demanded.

"The black widow eats its mate," I said, "and the others don't." I was tempted to ask if she had eaten Wil.

Then came the rattlesnake. It was about a foot long, coiled under an apricot tree and poised to strike. I couldn't hear its rattle for Aunt Emily's humming.

"You keep humming," I warned looking for a shovel, "and that sucker's going to go right after you. They're attracted by humming."

It was a masterstroke. She stopped humming instantly. I killed the snake, but reluctantly. It was a lousy way to repay anything that could mute Aunt Emily's hum.

I didn't know what might happen after that. Anything is possible when your luck is running bad.

I envisioned a giant owl carrying Emily off into the night, her skinny legs dangling out from under a black cotton dress. Or perhaps the puma which is rumored to prowl the mountains would make a sudden appearance, leaping down from the roof of the carport on to Aunt Emily's bony shoulders.

She was a lightning rod for minor catastrophes.

Aunt Emily was clearly not pleased with her experiences. I like the old broad and it pained me to feel she was not having a good time in L.A. Even the naked Jesus-loving neighbor who spoke loudly in tongues from his porch each evening did not amuse her.

I can understand the disappointment of coming to Southern California half expecting to see celebrities driving by in open-top convertibles and ending up instead in a canyon filled with rattlesnakes and black widows. The best I could offer was a friend who had once appeared on the "Gong Show" in a polar bear costume.

He sang "White Christmas."

SEX AND LAW

The question every lawyer in town is asking these days is whether the California state bar has any right to intrude on his sex life. Or her sex life.

It isn't a very profound question, but then lawyers are not profound people.

What is causing them consternation is a study under way by the bar's board of governors that could result in either the elimination or regulation of sex between attorneys and their clients.

The consideration stems not from a rush of conscience by the board, but as a result of pressure from Assemblywoman Lucille Roybal-Allard of Los Angeles.

She is author of a law that requires the bar to adopt a rule governing lawyer-client sex.

The subject has become so popular that even "L.A. Law" offered an episode on the debate, thus legitimizing its discussion in the real world.

My own interest in the bar's dilemma was precipitated by a conversation I overheard between two lawyers in a courthouse elevator.

One of them was saying it was nobody's business who, as he put it, his "sexual cohabitant" was. Lawyers talk that way. It's the party-of-the-first-part syndrome, or, in this case, the parties of the first and second parts.

Lawyer Number Two replied that it wasn't so much whether

they should have sex with clients, but whether they should charge them for the time it takes to achieve satisfaction.

The whole thing sounded a little like a Woody Allen movie, but I nevertheless began to wonder how seriously lawyers were taking the matter.

Of particular interest was a suggestion by one member of the board of governors that a client be advised of her rights *before* engaging in sex with her legal counselor.

It would require a lawyer to warn his prospective playmate in writing that joining him in what the French call *le sport* could have adverse effects.

The proposal doesn't specify what the adverse effects might be, but others have speculated it could mean erosion of a client's trust and reliance in her lawyer.

An attorney I spoke with named Max winked and said any client who had sex with him would emerge not only with vastly increased trust and reliance, but also with awesome respect.

Max is single and always on the alert for what he regards as sexual signals from women in his midst. He sees these signals in anything from a smile to a punch in the mouth.

Forget that some consider him slime and despise the ground he walks on, Max knows they would all really like to get him into the sack.

He is not unlike Richard Benjamin in *Diary of a Mad Housewife,* who never seemed quite able to perceive what was going on around him.

A woman attorney, Beverly, suggests that lawyers be furnished with a card they could hand a client before the sex act takes place.

Such a card would contain wording similar to that in the Miranda Rule, which advises suspects of their right to remain silent, etc.

In this case, it would be the right not to have sex with one's lawyer and warn of the potential for problems thereafter. The right to remain silent would not be an issue.

Another lawyer, Roger, said that while he has never personally "romped" with a client (*romped?*), it would not be a concern of the state bar if he did.

Allowing the bar to make these kinds of rules for them, he said, would be like having a third person in bed during coition, a practice of which he does not happen to approve.

"I don't need a member of the board of governors lying between me and my lover commenting on the propriety of my actions," he said. "If I'm going to do it, I'm going to do it."

Roger regards as "ethical foreplay" a further proposal that an attorney suggest a client get another lawyer if there is any possibility they might end up under the covers, or, in certain cases, under the desk.

"How would you know?" Roger demanded. "That kind of thing can happen pretty suddenly. One minute you're adjudicating and the next minute you're fornicating. There's no time to serve papers."

None of the attorneys I spoke with, by the way, wanted their names used.

"It is best," Max said grandly, "to keep me *in petto.*" According to my Latin phrase book, that means in secret.

I guess it really doesn't matter who lawyers have sex with, where they have it, how they have it or if they have it at all.

But if it keeps them away from cluttering the dockets with lawsuits, then I say *vive la bagatelle!* That's French. It means let the party of the first part enjoy the party of the second part, and I'll see you in court.

I CAN HEAR THE LAUGHTER

One sees him walking slowly across the sand of a sun-splashed beach, a little girl by the hand, looking back at the camera through eyes as blue as the surf.

He laughs and the camera lingers on his face the way memory clings to special moments, and then he turns back to the ocean and is gone, the silent laughter drifting toward the sea like a tendril of silver fog.

Chuck Meade was, by universal standards, an ordinary man. His name is not likely to grace the pages of history nor his image the walls of museums.

But in an age when hostilities abound and generation gaps widen, Meade lived his life with a triumph of spirit that made him special to at least one group of people in the world.

His family called him "Papa" and they loved him dearly.

I was introduced to Meade through a daughter, Michelene Reed of North Hollywood, who sent me a six-minute videotape that traces her father's life from photographs of his childhood to family movies of his old age.

She wrote, "You have been on my mind today because you're one of the enjoyments my father and I shared. . . .

"We often called each other up to ask, 'Did you read Al today?' and laugh like mad.

"My sweet papa died in the summer of Eighty-seven and I've just finished a video on him. Now I'd like you to meet him on tape. Al Martinez, this is Chuck Meade."

Newspapers allow scant space for average people, with the exception of those who fall victim to calamity.

Quiet summer natures provide warmth, but lightning in the soul creates drama, and drama is the stuff of headlines.

Michelene's letter made clear that the man she called Papa had died at age eighty-two without ever having led a parade, and my tendency was to answer with a thank-you note and let it go at that.

Then late one night, home from wandering, alone with my weariness, I watched the videotape she had sent me.

Here was Chuck Meade as a farm boy in Wisconsin, as a high school tumbler, as the husband of a dazzling young dancer, as a father with a growing family, as a dapper banker and business manager and, finally, as a gray-haired man handsome enough to be a movie star.

The tape, composed by Michelene and her fiance, is the kind of affectionate tribute few fathers are accorded, with a joy so real it projects beyond the television screen.

It was put together with special feeling.

We hear Chuck's voice telling a story of his grandparents' first Thanksgiving in America, and we see the compelling footage of a son who died in infancy, edging with faint sadness a tape otherwise made in celebration.

I watched it once and then twice: Meade pushing a daughter in a wheelbarrow, dancing with his wife, showing off a pet chicken, mowing a lawn, cooking at a family barbecue, blowing out birthday candles.

He was a gentle man who gave of himself with easy benevolence.

"I'll never stop missing him," Michelene said as we talked in her home a few days later. "I can still hear his laughter and see the twinkle in his eyes as he scolded us kids for egging the ice cream man.

"I can even remember the phone number of a store he owned in the forties. I was eight and he'd take me out of school and let me work for a day. It was the best time of my life." Pause. "Rugby 6-1905."

Chuck and Vasso Meade were married forty-eight years and

bore five children, who in turn gave them ten grandchildren.

Michelene describes him as an Irish charmer and a gentle tease, who loved to play the small tricks that kept the family laughing.

"But he was also a soft-hearted man," she said. "There was a story in the paper once of a boy who was very ill and Papa used to pray for him. When the boy died, Papa cried."

He told the children bedtime stories of his life on the farm when they were little and always sang one song to them, "The Animal Fair."

Nothing lasts forever. Summers pass, laughter fades and fathers die. But Meade, at the end, left the same warm glow he had provided in life, and this makes him special.

He suffered a stroke that left him barely able to speak. But he could still communicate as few can. With the family gathered by his bedside, he turned to them and sang, slowly and with strained articulation:

The animals had a fair, the birds and the beasts were there. . . .

"He sang it all the way through," Michelene said. "We laughed and cried at the same time. It was his way of saying he loved us."

A week later, Chuck Meade was dead. The videotape says good-bye in a loving manner to a father who achieved no cosmic heights but was adored by his family. And that, in its way, is triumph enough.

ARCHY GOES TO A ROAST

I felt like Archy the cockroach, viewing life from the underside.

In this case, however, it wasn't the physical grime of a New York alley, but the moral grime of a Friars Club celebrity roast in the Beverly Hilton Hotel.

You know what a roast is, other than being a hunk of meat.

A roast "honors" (their term) a person of note by ripping him or her to bloody shreds before a large audience and then, at the end, saying it was all in good fun, let's kiss and pray and laugh together.

I've only been to one of them, and that was a roast of Zsa Zsa Gabor the other night.

It was a dirty, mindless little performance by Milton Berle and a dozen or so others at the head table, during which scatological humor was elevated to the towering level of a dog's behind.

Zsa Zsa bore it all with a dim smile, and at the end responded at a level of articulation generally matching the intellectual quality of the evening.

I am told she suggested that the judge who sentenced her for slapping a cop should be made to clean toilets, a reference to her own sentence of one hundred and twenty hours of community service.

In a way, they were all cleaning toilets that night, and the thousand or so who paid one hundred and fifty dollars each to be there seemed oddly appreciative.

Only Archy and I, and maybe one or two others, were uncomfortable with what passes as humor in the private enclaves of show biz.

Archy, a philosopher and poet, was created by the late author-journalist Don Marquis in the early decades of this century.

The little cockroach wrote of New York's underbelly by hurling himself at the keys of a typewriter in the middle of the night in an abandoned newspaper city room.

The New York of which he wrote consisted of Mehitabel the cat and Broadway the lightning bug and a winsome moth who sought, for better or worse, the secret heart of a flame.

The underbelly of Hollywood, of which I write today, is brighter and cleaner and glitzier than the back alleys of Archy's days, but there's a kind of wretched sadness to it too.

Take that Friars Club roast.

We had an aging beauty queen of minimal talent being taunted by old-time comedians straining to recapture past glories through endless references to the human erogenous zones.

They should have held it at a Pussycat Theater.

I was there because, like Archy, it's my job to be at such desperate little gatherings, even when good sense dictates otherwise.

And, like Archy, I am no stranger to sexual humor.

I was raised on the streets of East Oakland, spent a hitch in the Marine Corps and began writing a newspaper column at a time when people like Lenny Bruce were redefining public obscenity as a weapon of social protest.

I even wrote a short story once about a couple who met and fell in love through an obscene telephone call.

All of those experiences contributed to my present ability to absorb the vilest kinds of comments relating to bodily functions. You want to talk dirty, fine, I'll talk dirty.

But not before an audience and not to rip the heart out of another human being in the name of humor.

I'm sure Archy felt the same way.

I didn't stay for the whole evening. I left shortly after the circumcision joke, or maybe it was the joke about the gorilla's

237

penis or about Zsa Zsa's sexual capacity, I can't remember.

It really didn't matter, because those I spoke with the next day said it was pretty much the same throughout.

Feminist Gloria Allred, the first woman admitted to Friars Club membership, called the evening racist, sexist, ageist, homophobic and anti-religious.

Veteran entertainment columnist Frank Swertlow said it was probably milder than other roasts he's attended, which leads me to wonder how bad these things really get.

Uncle Miltie, as Berle is often called, was the master of ceremonies, and from the outset left no doubt as to what the night would hold.

He began with a description of Gabor as the queen of you-probably-know-what. That precipitated a long, slow slide into the sewer which, apparently, is the trademark of the Friars.

If there was a redeeming quality to an evening like that, it was its intent to raise one hundred thousand dollars for the homeless, which I guess it did easily, judging from the size of the audience.

As Archy once wrote, "coarse jocosity catches the crowd."

But even coarse jocosity ought to have self-imposed limits.

VISIT TO A SMALL PLANET

He calls himself bobby BIBLE, lower case "bobby," all-caps "BIBLE." He would not give me his real name, not on your life, because the homosexuals would just love to track him down and get their paws on him. I'm not sure why, but that's what he said.

I found him outside the county courthouse building in which five anti-abortion activists were being tried for trespassing and other misdemeanors. Among them was Randall Terry, founder of Operation Rescue.

Normally I wouldn't stop and talk to a guy shouting "Jesus!" on a street corner, but since the anti-abortionists have been parading God through L.A. like a circus elephant, I felt it appropriate.

If not typical of their soldiers, Bible is certainly on their side. I'm not going to comply with his special name spellings, by the way, because that runs contrary to our style. I'm sure God would understand.

At any rate, there was something compelling about Bible. Dressed in striped shorts, sandals and two hats, one atop the other, he would alternately shout his anti-abortion message and whistle a Sunday school song, "Jesus Loves All the Little Children."

Sometimes he would whistle while standing on one foot, hoisting a large sign up and down in rhythm to the tune. The

sign said WITCHES, LESBIANS AND BASIC IDIOTS. REPENT. NO
CHOICE EXISTS IN MURDER. HEB. 9.

Bible, by the way, was born and raised in L.A., but you probably suspected that.

I had gone to the courthouse not to interview street preachers but to see what kind of people municipal judge Richard Paez and the Los Angeles visitors bureau had to deal with.

Randall Terry answered the first question by calling America's judiciary "the lap dog of the death industry," and his followers answered the second by distributing pamphlets calling L.A. "a true mother of harlots."

The pamphlet went on to say, "Preaching a dark gospel of adultery, divorce and total contempt for Christian moral standards and beliefs, (L.A.) radiates her fascination with violence, death, promiscuous sex and mindless materialism."

I hear you say, "Oh, not that again," but don't dismiss the paragraph out of hand.

Almost fifty million tourists visit the Mother of Harlots each year, and it's tough enough keeping them happy without luring another fifty million to our doorstep. There is nothing more enticing to the folks in Wichita than promiscuous sex and mindless materialism.

Approached properly, they can be more fun than Disneyland.

Of course, there are always people like Randall Terry and bobby Bible out there teaching the Mother of Harlots (can I call her mom?) a lesson she'll never forget, Randy working the crowd on the inside and bobby taking care of the street.

The day I checked out the trial, Bible was the only demonstrator, but he was a one-man band.

"Randall Terry and Operation Rescue are innocent, everyone else is guilty for allowing babies to be murdered!" he'd shout between whistles. It was a tough interview, because he would suddenly interrupt his answers to holler at a passer-by.

For instance, I'd ask, "Are you married, Bobby?"

He'd reply, "No, I'm fifty years old *(Will it be heaven or hell when you die?)* and a eunuch."

I asked him the same question twice because I couldn't believe he said he was a eunuch. Then he explained that some men emasculate themselves to become eunuchs and others are eunuchs by name. Bobby was of the latter group.

There was no question in my mind that Bible was anti-abortion, but I still wondered why he would take an expression of his viewpoint to such untoward extremes.

Not many would bare their chest and bellow damnation across from Rothschild's Bar and Grill.

"I'm doing God's work," he said. "Whoever serves God here, gets a better job in heaven."

"What kind of job would that be?"

"Well," Bobby said, "I thought maybe I'd *(Do you believe in God and life everlasting?)* be the manager of a planet."

He went on to explain that heaven is composed of several planets, each of which fulfills a specific need.

A recreational planet, for instance, would offer horseback riding, tennis, golf, big band music and maybe electronic game parlors for surly teenagers. Sorry, there are no whorehouses in heaven. They are all in L.A.

"Well, Bobby," I said, "good luck in your secular life and wherever else you might end up."

"Thanks," he said. "Maybe we'll *(Stop murdering babies!)* talk again someday."

Not on my planet we won't.

241

LOVE IN THE LIGHT

His words, fired in barrages of grief and anger, were an odd contradiction to the serenity of the afternoon, like war in the ebullience of spring.

He said he had two years to live, five at the most, as sunlight filtered through the trees of his quiet yard, touching the amber petals of bougainvillea that cascaded over a low wall.

"I bury someone almost every two weeks," he was saying, "and that has gone on for years. At least two hundred of my friends have died."

I remember being aware of life's affirmations as he spoke, the far-off barking of a dog, the soft whack of a hammer on wood, the trill of a bird.

And I remember looking at the man, so alive with rage and talent, and wondering precisely what fears burned like magnesium in the darkest corners of his soul.

What heed to the ticking clock does he pay in the quiet hours of night when a brutal awareness of his own mortality flashes across the face of insomnia?

Four hundred years ago John Dryden wrote, "All human things are subject to decay, and when fate summons, monarchs must obey."

But the intrusion of disease through an immune system that has failed is not the best way to die.

This is as much a column about me as it is Paul Monette, in

whose West Hollywood garden we sat that sunny afternoon.

Monette, forty-four, is a gay man and a gifted writer who has tested positive for the human immunodeficiency virus, or HIV, the precursor of AIDS.

He lives, he says, in a surrealistic world—"on the moon," he calls it—where time and reality are distorted by one's vibrant awareness of life, and the shadowy proximity of death.

It was through this man that I came face to face with a prejudice so ingrained in my generation that it is almost invisible, the way small flowers pale in comparison to the abundance in Paul's garden.

It has taken me a while to face it.

I am not a man without compassion, despite small angers that surface within the boundaries of my work.

I have wondered with growing discomfort why so gentle an emotion as love should have released so deadly a plague as AIDS, and I bristle at the notion of God's vengeance.

But, still, I have done little in this space to convey my own growing horror toward a disease that has killed three hundred thousand people in the world since 1980.

Why haven't I employed this forum to clang alarm bells down Spring Street and into the valleys and canyons, and toward the clustered communities of the desert?

I can only blame that reluctance on a prejudice planted without hostility by those who shaped my attitudes with the same clay passed on by their progenitors.

They are them, we said, and we are us. We drank to that difference with indifference, and watched from the safety of our own sexual orientation the shadows that fell over another.

This began to change for me when I came across Monette's book. It is called *Borrowed Time,* and is about the death of his "beloved friend" for ten years, Roger Horowitz.

Horowitz died of AIDS in 1986. *Borrowed Time* is not only a haunting chronicle of the years Paul and Roger spent together, but a history of the "gay cancer," whose fatal cells continue to creep insidiously around the globe.

Few books I have ever read are more compelling or more

beautifully composed than this. *Borrowed Time* is simultaneously full of sorrow and love, and a pain of loss that claws at the heart.

Where once I might have thought of love between two men as a disquieting anomaly, I can only think of it now in terms of the feeling Paul and Roger must have had for one another.

Was it any less than mine for my Joanne?

"I am only saying," Monette writes, "that I loved him. . . . (and) . . . that love became the only untouched shade in the dawning fireball."

It was after I read *Borrowed Time* that I sat with Monette in the filtered sunlight of his backyard and listened to his rage of grief and loss, directed now toward the indifference that continues to characterize the spread of AIDS.

"We all have a lot of re-learning and evolving to do," Monette said, as a soft breeze stirred the petals of the flowers. "The most we can achieve is to understand that all men are our brothers."

What I have come to understand, I guess, is that Paul's pain is my pain, and his grief my grief. What we own, we own together and what we lose, we lose together.

The man grows older, but the man keeps learning. We are indeed brothers, and it's time I took my brother's hand.

WILL WORK FOR COLUMN

She looked like one of the Joads in *The Grapes of Wrath,* or maybe a brave country woman trying to save her farm. Call her Beth.

I noticed her parked along the ocean, sitting on a folding chair by an old camper, holding a sign that said, WILL WORK FOR GAS.

A girl about ten stood next to her in a pose out of a Grant Wood painting. She had one hand on her mother's shoulder and was staring out at the passing traffic with the kind of sad-sweet look that could melt glaciers.

She reminded me of Tatum O'Neal selling bibles in *Paper Moon.*

I stopped because I've been doing a sort of survey on people who hold will-work-for signs. Will work for food. Will work for gas. Will work.

What they want, of course, is not to work at all but to have you give them money so they won't have to. It's a nice idea, but not the way the system is supposed to function.

Of a half-dozen will-work men I talked to, not one wanted the job I offered. I said I'd pay five dollars an hour for digging with a pick and shovel.

One said it wasn't his kind of work. His kind of work was playing the flute. When I said I had no work for flautists but would still pay him for digging, he passed.

When I left without giving him money, he gave me something: the finger.

I swear I'd seen Beth before, and her little girl too. A mother and daughter approached me by a bank machine once and said they were from Fresno and were trying to raise money to get home.

It had scam written all over it. I said, "Why would anyone want to go to Fresno?"

My response caught her off-guard for a moment. Then she realized I was a wise ass non-giver and her look of helpless vulnerability sharpened to piercing hostility.

Without saying another word, she jerked the little girl by the arm and headed off down the block, half-dragging the kid with her.

When I mentioned to Beth that she looked like a woman from Fresno, there was a flicker of apprehension in her eyes, but she recovered quickly and said she'd never been to Fresno. She kept looking at me as though she were trying to remember who I was.

"Where are you going?" I asked.

"Nowhere in particular," she said.

"Where've you been?"

"Here and there."

"What's your name?" I asked the child.

"She don't talk," Beth said quickly. Then: "You a cop?"

I told her I was a journalist. She said she didn't have time to answer questions unless I was willing to pay.

The little girl was looking at me all this time as though she had something to say but didn't dare say it.

She may have been playacting, the way Tatum was, but there's still a sweetness to children that can't be denied. That's why they're used so often in con games.

"We don't pay for stories," I said, "but I'll give you five dollars if you let me look in your camper."

She rose, closed the folding chair and said, "Let's go" to the kid.

The girl lingered for a moment and I slipped her the five

anyhow. She touched my hand momentarily, half-smiled and was gone.

I keep remembering that touch.

There's no doubt in my mind it was a scam. Santa Monica Police Sergeant John Miehle, who knows about these things, said I was right.

"Some of those people make fortunes," he said. "One guy stands at the corner of Lincoln and Olympic with a will-work sign. He's there every day. That's his job.

"Three hundred thousand cars pass that intersection during a twenty-four-hour period. If the guy gets a dollar from one-tenth of one percent of those cars, he's making three hundred dollars a day. Why should he do anything else?"

One couple, a man and woman, wait until parking lots close for the day and are free, and stand at the entryway, collecting parking fees.

Others hang around gas stations where you don't have to pay before you pump. They put gasoline in the cars of customers, collect the money and split.

The will-work signs began popping up about a year ago. Miehle checked out one sign-carrier who carried a wad of money the size of a baseball. He'd gotten it from people who can't offer a job but can't stand to see anyone hungry, either. So they give a buck.

Miehle says don't give money to individuals, give it to social service organizations. He's right, I guess.

I shouldn't have given the kid the fiver. She probably threw it in mama's barrel with a hundred other fives or bought beer with it, but what the hell.

The touch of a child's hand is more powerful than a man's fist. Maybe she'll remember me someday on the long, lonely road to nowhere-in-particular.

NOTING A NEW BORDER

I give my wife a Mother's Day present every year. I realize she's not my mother, but it's a good opportunity to buy her something she needs. This year, for instance, I gave her two Mexicans.

She was, of course, grateful. "Now," she said cheerfully, "I have three."

I gave her the Mexicans because the yard is filled with weeds, because Anglos won't do that kind of work and because I'm not going to be a party to establishing a new border.

As Desi Arnaz used to say, let me 'splain.

This has not been a good year for Mexicans. First, Fernando Valenzuela got the boot, then the mayor of suburban Culver City called for closing the border between the U.S. and Mexico, and now various communities in the county are at war with day workers who gather on street corners hoping to be hired.

The communities are demanding, in effect, that a new border be established. This one would protect Us from Them.

While an ethnic umbilical may link me to Latinos, there's nothing personal in my sympathy toward those under fire for seeking a better life.

That's what we're all about, isn't it? Give me your tired, your poor, your huddled masses. . . . was never intended to apply to whites only.

It doesn't say keep the wretched refuse on your teeming

shores and send us Swedes and Danes. It just says welcome to the melting pot, everybody.

Unfortunately, however, the melting pot hasn't been all that gracious lately. For instance, when I went down to get the two Mexicans for my wife, I think I was being videotaped.

This is part of a campaign in Topanga to discourage anyone from hiring day workers. The idea is to turn the tape over to the immigration service so those who employ illegals can be fined, and possibly tortured.

The reason they're doing this, say the video vigilantes, is that many of the Mexicans camp in the mountains, thus increasing the danger of fire, theft, vandalism, drunkenness, indecent exposure and all the other crimes generally attributed to brown people.

Opponents of the vigilantes are of the opposite persuasion. Given the opportunity, they would establish soup kitchens and brothels to fill whatever need the workers seem to manifest, in exchange for which the workers would promise not to marry their sisters.

These opponents argue that the motivation of the video vigilante is a combination of racism and greed. They simultaneously dislike Mexicans and fear property values will come tumbling down if word gets around that the community is infested with them.

Malibu, the Capital of Blond, had the same problem with its hiring center and shut it down. It wasn't so much the fire danger as the penetrating aroma of chili that rankled those who opposed the center.

Everyone knows, of course, that chili fumes, like ultraviolet rays, have an adverse effect on the complexion of light-skinned dudes who live near the ocean. And when humanity intrudes on dermatology, it's adios, bracero.

In Santa Clarita, the city council did a quick flip. It started out considering a proposal to build a hiring center and ended up urging the INS to round up the day workers and deport them to Mexico.

Not exactly what the workers expected, but he who swims with sharks runs the risk of being eaten.

I mentioned the mayor of Culver City. His name is Steven Gourley. He's a forty-two-year-old lawyer who'll tell you right off, by way of establishing his liberal credentials, that he loves God, Abraham Lincoln and Harry Truman.

But what he told the city council a few weeks back is, "If George Bush wants to draw a line in the sand, he should draw a line between Tijuana and San Diego."

Gourley, now ex-mayor, explained later that it wasn't a question of disliking Mexicans, but of wanting to relieve the burden of America's overtaxed social services. Our system, he said, is breaking down. Ergo, don't fix the system, close the border.

Then who'd pull our weeds? I offered three different Anglo homeless people six dollars an hour to do light yard work. They all carried WILL WORK signs, and they all refused.

One said he couldn't due to "bad psychology." Another called me a smartass and walked away. A woman suggested there might be other ways to please me beside pulling weeds.

So much for the wretched refuse of our own teeming shore.

I asked the Mexicans I hired for my wife what they thought of all this. They were both named Jose, so we called them Jose One and Jose Two.

Jose One smiled and said "Sure." It was less an affirmation of principle than a lack of communication. He didn't speak English.

Jose Two was more philosophical. He shrugged and said, "They don't like Mexicans, I guess."

I guess. But they've got three of us on videotape now, amigo, and I don't think it's for a sequel to *La Bamba*.

DEATH, TAXES AND PANTIES

The only certainties in life, as everyone knows, are death and taxes. That is to say, they have been the only certainties in life until now.

Today I offer a third. Death, taxes and the assurance that women employees in the Bank of America are wearing panties.

Well, anyhow, they're supposed to.

I get my information by way of history's most reliable source of troublemaking: a disgruntled employee.

The willingness of disgruntled employees to tell all has always been an accepted method of toppling governments, exposing fraud and ending religious crusades.

But I don't think one of them has ever been involved in the area of human underwear before.

Call my source Holly. She is no longer with the bank, but she did furnish me a copy of the dress code given to all employees.

Item one under the category for women: "Undergarments: Bra, slip, panties and nylons are a must at all times."

And if you're not wearing them, you'll be sent home to get them.

This naturally raises a question. While it may or may not be apparent that a female employee isn't wearing a bra or a slip, how will anyone know she isn't wearing panties?

Has the Bank of America hired what feminist Gloria Allred calls panty police?

Holly was given the dress code by a branch officer she knew as Becky. So I called her.

Becky answered the telephone in the rigidly cheerful manner that has come to characterize large institutions with Our Best Interests at Heart.

When I told her who I was, the cheer lessened slightly. When I told her what I wanted, it hissed from her attitude like air from a child's balloon.

"What is it you want to know?" she asked cautiously.

"I'd like to know who checks to see whether or not your female employees are wearing panties."

"You will have to talk to our area manager, Mr. Pat Leaver," she said.

"He's the one who checks?"

"You will have to talk to Mr. Leaver for information," she said.

Click.

Pat Leaver thought the dress code a little more . . . well . . . specific than most.

"Generally," he said, "our standard is shirts and ties for the men and"—he mumbled a bit here—"we ask that women wear hose and bras."

Leaver is district operations manager for the West San Fernando Valley. He is a friendly gee-and-gosh kind of guy. One imagines him smiling and scuffing at the dirt as he speaks.

"I don't know about the underpants," he said, a little embarrassed. "They must have had an incident that prompted that."

"A pants-less incident?" I suggested helpfully.

"Bra-less maybe," he said.

If I were casting a movie about Pat Leaver, he'd have to be a young Jimmy Stewart.

"How would you check a thing like that?" he wondered aloud in reference to the panty code.

"I was going to ask you that," I said.

"Golly, I don't know."

Individual branches can establish their own dress code as

252

long as they are within the parameters of common decency and good taste. Like pornography, local custom prevails.

"They might not have the same dress code in Malibu that they have downtown," Leaver said. "In fact, they used to wear swimsuits under their clothes in Malibu so they could go to the beach during their lunch hours."

He didn't know of any other branch, however, where panties were an issue.

"They really have that kind of dress code?" Gloria Allred said, salivating. "That's an outright invasion of privacy."

Everyone knows Gloria. Get kicked out of a restaurant for nursing your kid and Gloria is there. Get booted off a cheer-leading squad for having big boobs and Gloria comes sweeping out of the night.

She is to sexism what the Pope is to sin, a mortal enemy.

"Does the bank insist men wear shorts?" she demanded when I told her about the dress code.

Negative. The only intimate attire for men that is mentioned is socks.

"Then it's blatant sexism," Gloria said.

I love it when she snorts and paws the ground.

"Dress codes are so dated it boggles the mind," she said. "Bank of America must have invested in panties. Are they opening factories?"

Then she added darkly, "I wonder how the men on the corporate board would feel about having their underwear regulated?"

I don't know about them, but I know that Holly sure didn't like it. She stayed at the bank for three weeks then quit. She didn't wear panties the last day, but no one checked. This being L.A., the official panty-checker was probably down at the beach, dancing under the sun.

DEALING WITH MISS ETHEL

My wife was in the hospital recently for some relatively minor surgery and it made a nervous wreck out of me.

I do not say that lightly. The only obvious genetic traits passed down by my parents were my father's short legs and my mother's towering ability to worry.

So I paced the lobby of Tarzana Medical Center on my little short legs all during my wife's surgery and worried myself into a frenzy.

Mom, had she not worried herself to death, would have been proud.

It occurred to me, however, on the fifth circle of the lobby that I had to do something to alleviate the stress. It isn't easy pacing on short legs.

I thought about having a martini, but that probably wasn't a good idea at that time of the morning and under those circumstances.

The hospital did not provide a cocktail lounge and I will not drink in bars that open at 6 A.M. I have principles.

My second response to stress is to read. So I went into the hospital gift shop.

Hospital gift shops, for those who have not visited them lately, are the province of old ladies with time on their hands. I met one of them on this day.

I could not quite read her name tag, so I am guessing when

I say her name was Ethel. She was somewhere in her mid-seventies, maybe older.

When I selected a book, a pot of flowers and some newspapers, Ethel said, "That's all you want?" There was a tone of incredulity in her voice.

"Is there something else I ought to be buying?"

"Suit yourself," she said.

Worry makes me snappish. Ethel was maybe four-feet-nine and nearsighted. I could have taken her in a fair fight, but it wouldn't have been right.

"What credit cards do you take?" I asked.

"Cash," Ethel said firmly. "I need cash. This isn't the Miami Hilton."

"I don't have cash," I said. "I have credit cards. Everyone takes credit cards. Cash is going out of style."

"I don't have change," Ethel said.

That was my first indication Ethel and I were operating on different levels.

"You don't need change with credit cards," I said.

"I shouldn't even be here," Ethel said. "It's not my day. I don't know why I'm here."

I took it Ethel was a volunteer and had been brought in on an emergency basis. She wasn't happy about it.

"How about a check?" I said.

"Is it good?" she asked. "Don't get me into trouble."

"It's good," I said.

"Don't get me into trouble," she said again.

I wrote the check and handed Ethel my driver's license and a Citibank Visa as a matter of habit.

"I don't take credit cards," Ethel said.

"It's for identification."

"My son works for Citibank," Ethel said. "He's only forty-two and he's a vice president."

She studied me in the manner of someone looking at a man who is over forty-two and not a vice president. What went wrong?

Then she said, "This card's no good. It expired in March."

"No," I said, "that's when the period started. See?" I pointed. " 'Valid from 03/01/89 to 02/91.' "

"Don't get me into trouble," she said. "I'm not even supposed to be here."

"The check is good," I said. "You're in safe hands."

"Your driver's license has expired!" she said suddenly. "It hasn't been good for four years!"

I handed her a renewal card that indicated the expiration date had been extended.

"It's good until July," I said triumphantly.

"Well," she said, "the picture doesn't look like you."

"Ethel," I said, impatience creeping into my voice, "how long have you been doing this?"

"Who knows?" she said. "Forever. I need some other identification. I'm suspicious about the picture."

I handed her my *L.A. Times* ID card. It is a card I use rarely as ultimate proof of my worth and my existence. Only a media pass to Vatican City is more impressive.

"Most doctors read the *Herald Examiner*," Ethel said, studying the card. "It has more bad news. Doctors like bad news. What do you do?"

"I'm a nude model," I said. "Just OK the check so I can get out of here."

About then, I heard myself being paged. I left the gift shop with Ethel watching me suspiciously.

"Where've you been?" an angry old man at the front desk demanded. "This is the third time you've been paged."

Ethel had followed me across the lobby. "You didn't sign your check," she said. "I *knew* there was something wrong!"

My wife was fine. I was exhausted.

SWEET BYPASS BLUES

I am lying in a bed at Good Samaritan Hospital in one of those gowns that does not cover your behind, when a medical assistant at the foot of my bed says, "OK, let's go." I say, "I've changed my mind."

"Sure you have," he says, loading me onto a gurney. I have already been sedated so I have no strength to rise up and punch him in the mouth, which is my tendency.

"One of these days," I say to my wife, Cinelli, as they wheel me down the hall toward surgery, "I am going to come back and beat the crap out of him."

She is walking beside me holding my hand, as she has always held my hand when times have not been good for me.

"He's pretty big," she whispers. "Maybe you should just plan on *writing* the crap out of him."

I am sinking deeper into a kind of twilight world, but I do remember thinking as we approach the operating room there are familiar elements here for something creative, but I can't focus on what that might be.

My surgeon is a preppy young doctor from a famous family; another cardiologist is a cute, perky woman with a Peter Pan haircut. A third is a French-Canadian with Paul Newman eyes, and the anesthesiologist is a hip, black guy who wears a gold chain around his neck and speaks jive.

Then it hits me. "My God," I say to Cinelli, half-rising from the gurney, "this is a television series and they're wheeling me onto a sound stage."

"I'll call your agent," she says, kissing me gently. Tears shine in her eyes. The door of the operating room opens.

"I wonder if I'll be any taller," I call back, as the world I knew before closes behind me. "They say some people get taller after a bypass. . . . "

I did not come casually to this moment. I hurtled downhill from a place where I smoked cigarettes, drank martinis, ate cows and floated in seas of sauces and whipped cream.

Two of my arteries were clogged and they weren't going to get suddenly unclogged. Miracles don't work for me. That was proved beyond doubt when Cinelli and I spent overnight in Lourdes once while driving through France. Where others were being cured at the grotto, I got the flu.

I remember Cinelli saying, "I don't know what somebody's trying to tell you, but I wouldn't ever count on God or Bernadette for quick cures if I were you."

"It's no screaming emergency," the surgeon at Good Sam was saying, "but don't wait until Christmas to have it done."

"All right," I said, "let's do it." I felt like Walter Mitty before the firing squad. *To hell with the blindfold.*

"Just one thing," I said to the cardiologist. "No Country-Western music."

I had just seen the film *The Doctor,* in which the cardiologist performed surgery to a background of shit-kickin' music. If anything went wrong, I didn't want to die with "Okie From Muskogee" running through my fading subconscious.

"I don't do the procedure to music," he said, peering at me through round, wire-rimmed glasses.

When he left I turned to Cinelli. "Thank God, it's a procedure, not actual surgery where they have to cut you open."

"You keep bugging them," she said, "it'll be a barbecue."

The surgery, I mean procedure, involved three major risks, the cardiologist with the Peter Pan haircut had said to me earlier. I don't remember the other two, but one of them was death.

"We have to say that," she said, "but I don't think it will be a problem in your case."

She was right. I emerged from the anesthesia cursing the tubes in my nose, my chest and in other areas I choose not to mention. There is a healing quality to rage. I will not go gentle into that good night.

Also, I did not hallucinate, which was supposed to be a postprocedural problem. At least I don't think I did. Sometimes I'm not sure where reality ends and hallucinations begin. That's why they made me a columnist.

Was I afraid? Everyone's afraid of something. Darkness, pain, memories, the thought of Jerry Brown somehow winning the presidency. My only fear is that I might actually learn to like tofu.

I don't mean to minimize heart bypasses. It's serious business and should not be tried at home on your little friends.

But it's over for me, and I feel like an old alley cat, back prowling the streets again. You helped. You send cards and left phone messages. You said, "Come back, old alley cat. Dance under the moon again."

I've been given another chance, one more dance in L.A. It's a kind of renewal, so I'll end this column the way I ended the first I ever wrote, with one variation:

Good morning. My name is Martinez. I write. *Still.*